PLANNING FOR
COASTAL RESILIENCE

PLANNING
FOR COASTAL
RESILIENCE

BEST PRACTICES

FOR CALAMITOUS TIMES

Timothy Beatley

ISLANDPRESS

WASHINGTON | COVELO | LONDON

Library of Congress Cataloging-in-Publication Data

Beatley, Timothy, 1957-
  Planning for coastal resilience : best practices for calamitous times / Timothy
Beatley.
     p. cm.
  Includes bibliographical references and index.
  ISBN-13: 978-1-59726-561-4 (cloth : alk. paper)
  ISBN-10: 1-59726-561-6 (cloth : alk. paper)
  ISBN-13: 978-1-59726-562-1 (pbk. : alk. paper)
  ISBN-10: 1-59726-562-4 (pbk. : alk. paper) 1. Coastal management--United
States. 2. Sustainable development--United States. 3. Emergency management-
-United States. I. Title.
  HT392.B47 2009
  333.91'7160973--dc22

                                                            2008045216

Printed on recycled, acid-free paper ⊕

Design by Joan Wolbier

Manufactured in the United States of America
10 9 8 7 6 5 4 3 2 1

CONTENTS

ACKNOWLEDGMENTS

THIS BOOK RESULTS FROM A GENEROUS grant from the National Oceanic and Atmospheric Administration Coastal Services Center, in Charleston, South Carolina. I am especially thankful to the director, Margaret Davidson and the center for the resources and helpful guidance along the way in preparing this manuscript. In particular, I wish to thank the center project officer, Kelly Dickson, who provided significant support and invaluable guidance along the way. Her suggestions related to both editing and content have made what follows a much stronger book.

In developing the case studies for this book, I consulted a number of colleagues in the coastal management and planning field, and I wish to thank them for their suggestions and advice. These include Phil Berke, Sam Brody, David Brower, Ray Burby, Robert Deyle, Robert Freitag, Jack Kartez, André LeDuc, Robert Olshansky, Orrin Pilkey, and Rutherford Platt.

Several graduate students in the Urban and Environmental Planning Department at the University of Virginia worked on aspects of this book. In particular, Shawn Means and Javier del Castillo conducted research and developed bibliographic materials for the project, and Javier prepared several of the tables to follow. Many individuals provided time and information in the preparation of the coastal resilience case studies contained in the latter chapters of the book. While too numerous to mention here, I am very thankful for their willingness to help and to speak so caringly of their respective communities, and for their commitment to making their communities more resilient.

The work that follows in exploring the practical and planning implications of resilience for coastal management follows in the footsteps of others. Notable is the early and important work of Professor David Godschalk, at the University of North Carolina at Chapel Hill. His important paper on urban resilience has been an inspiration for many of us working on this topic.

ACKNOWLEDGMENTS

As usual, I received the enthusiastic support and excellent editing of Heather Boyer at Island Press. Finally, I would like to thank my family for their loving support and generous patience during the researching and writing of this book. All mistakes or misstatements herein are, of course, mine alone.

INTRODUCTION

Climate Change and Coastal Resilience

WE ARE DRAWN, IT SEEMS, EMOTIONALLY and economically, to the edge of land, where sea and sand meet, and where terra firma gives way to the vastness of ocean and marine habitats. Coastal environments are highly productive ecologically, and historically we have been interested in them as a matter of navigational and commercial necessity. The very history of this nation began with coastal cities like Boston, New York, and Charleston—places that offered economic opportunities and facilitated the settlement and growth of the nation as a whole. We are drawn, moreover, to coastal environments for their beauty, mystery, and wonder, and we should not minimize the emotional value and connectedness we derive from these places. However, in light of current trends and future pressures, we will have to find new ways to live in and with the coast, new ways of reconciling the desire to be near it with the cautious humility and respect for the dangers a changing climate will present. Our coastal management strategy increasingly will need to be based less on armoring, less on conventional large-project infrastructure, and more on resilience and adaptability.

As the full effects of climate change become manifest, coastal cities and regions will face a range of increasingly severe challenges. To effectively plan for and respond to these challenges will require new ways of thinking and working. This book argues that all future coastal planning and management must reflect a commitment to the concept of resilience. Indeed coastal resilience must become the primary design and planning principle that guides all future development and all future growth and infrastructure decisions.

Climate change is perhaps our planet's gravest threat and challenge, and coastal communities are where the full brunt and impact of the predicted physical changes will be the greatest. The Fourth Assessment Report of the Intergovernmental Panel on Climate Change (IPCC), released in 2007, paints a dire and calamitous future, with special impacts for coastal environments. Average global temperatures have already risen 1.4 degrees Fahrenheit (0.8 degree Celsius) since the industrial period began, but much more is in store. If we continue down the "business as usual" path of heavy reliance on fossil fuels, we are likely to see temperatures increase by some 7 degrees Fahrenheit (4 degrees Celsius) by the end of the century (IPCC 2007a, 13). The implications for coastal communities and regions are severe and many. Sea levels have already been rising (the Atlantic coast has experienced about 1 foot [ca. 0.33 meter] of increase over the last hundred years), with higher rates likely. The IPCC predicts that global sea levels will rise between 7 inches and 1.9 feet (0.18–0.58 meter) by the end of the twenty-first century (IPCC, 2007a, 13); many, however, believe these estimates to be conservative, and not fully reflective of the dynamics of glacial and ice shelf melting. The signals there are not very positive, with substantial increases in the extent of summer melting of the Greenland Ice Sheet in recent years. The news from Canada has also not been good: the problem of its shrinking ice shelves was given further urgency by the dramatic breaking off of the massive Markham Ice Shelf in August 2008. While even conservative predictions of sea level rise are worrisome, when the potential effects of melting—especially of the Greenland and West Antarctic ice sheets—are taken into account, an even more catastrophic sea level rise—on the order of multiple meters—must be confronted. Jim Hansen, director of the National Aeronautics and Space Administration's Goddard Institute for Space Studies argues that, based on Earth's history, a 25-meter (82-foot) sea level rise is conceivable, given what we know about sea levels 3 million years ago (the last time it was as hot as it will likely be under the business-as-usual scenario; see, e.g., Hansen 2007). Perhaps Hansen is overly pessimistic (and overcompensating for what he believes is the inherent conservatism of science), but the scenario is clearly within the realm of possibility. Even a few meters' sea level rise will have dramatic impacts on our coastlines, coastal commerce, and way of life.

Sea level rise is, of course, not the only impact of climate change that coastal communities need to anticipate. There is increasingly reliable evidence that the frequency and magnitude of coastal storms and hurricanes will rise. A recent study by researchers at Florida State University, for instance, concludes that the strongest tropical cyclones, as measured by wind speeds, are getting ever stronger over time

(FSU 2008). The increase in wind speed is likely a function of the heat energy effects of warming sea waters, but it suggests that coastal planners must anticipate and plan for even more difficult preparedness, evacuation, and damage loss scenarios. More people and property as well as environmental and community assets will be impacted by these events, and coastal leaders must be ready. Stronger, more frequent hurricanes and coastal storms will challenge the normalcy of coastal living and cause immense economic, social, and environmental disruption.

Coastal communities will be forced to simultaneously plan for and tackle the potentially episodic and catastrophic effects of larger, more frequent storms while moving expeditiously to address longer-term adaptations to a changing climate— for example, moving back from shorelines; moving up and out of the most dangerous coastal locations; and preparing for heat waves, water shortages, and increased air pollution. The agenda is daunting: planners must keep in mind and move forward on multiple serious challenges that also must be tracked on different time scales. Resiliency offers a useful framework, as this book argues, for integrating these different challenges with policy and planning agendas.

These significant changes in physical dangers are accompanied by urbanization patterns and population and development pressures that are placing ever more people and property in harm's way. Because these development patterns impact and disrupt the ecological patterns of natural systems, the ability of coastal environments to mitigate and absorb the likely impacts of flooding, storms, and sea level rise is lessened, further contributing to increasing levels of coastal vulnerability. The replacement of wetlands, forests, and farm fields with roadways, rooftops, and impervious urban hardscapes is a recipe for increased coastal flooding. At precisely the time when coastal communities and regions need to take advantage of the full mitigative benefits and resilience values provided by healthy ecological systems, these systems have been degraded and diminished.

Coastal communities have always faced formidable preparedness and disaster management issues—for example, when to call for evacuation in the face of an impending hurricane or tropical storm, and ensuring that the necessary roadways and infrastructure to permit such an evacuation are in place. In addition, many coastal communities have faced pressing environmental resource management problems, such as ensuring adequate water supply and protecting the water quality in bay, estuarine, and nearshore coastal waters. These matters have been perennial concerns and planning and management challenges, of course, but climate change promises to profoundly expand and exacerbate these problems.

While the image of a small coastal resort community is an accurate one along many parts of the U.S. coast, coastal management is more often a matter of dealing with the problems of coastal cities and dense urban settlements. Normal urban problems—such as air pollution; excessive highway construction and car dependence; waste management; and the massive challenges of delivering a host of services and infrastructure from energy to wastewater collection, wastewater treatment, and water supply—become even more severe and more pressing when the likely impacts of climate change are added to them. There is evidence, for instance, that ozone levels in coastal cities like New York will increase in response to rising temperatures along the East Coast. Heat waves and periods of severe drought will exacerbate both water supply and water quality issues. The higher summer temperatures that eastern coastal cities will face raise significant public health and safety concerns, especially for the elderly (a growing demographic category). Climate change in the face of increasing urbanization threatens to exacerbate all these problems as well as to introduce new ones.

The problem of designing and planning coastal cities in the face of climate change is a daunting one. Evidence suggests that coastal cities around the world are growing faster than their noncoastal counterparts and are already denser. A combination of sharp increases in coastal urbanization and population growth and increasingly severe climate events will place ever more people at risk. A recent global analysis of population patterns estimates that there are 634 million people living in locations less than 10 meters (33 feet) above sea level. According to McGranahan, Balk, and Anderson (2007, 22) 10 percent of the world's population lives within these so-called low-elevation coastal zone (LECZ) areas, which amount to but 2 percent of the world's land. While the percentage of the U.S. population living in such especially high-risk zones is lower than the percentage of the corresponding population in many other countries (e.g., consider Bangladesh and Vietnam, with 46 percent and 55 percent respectively), the absolute number of people and the extent of the land area vulnerable are very large indeed (about 22.8 million people and 235,000 square kilometers [ca. 90,000 square miles]). The United States has the third-largest amount of land below this 10-meter (33-foot) level (preceded only by Russia and Canada; see McGranahan, Balk, and Anderson 2007, 29).

That there are tremendous economic ramifications to these trends and predictions is an understatement. The U.S. coastline contains billions of dollars in property and infrastructure. A recent study (Nicholls et al. 2007) of the likely increased flood damages in port cities around the world finds a striking increase in assets and wealth at risk: the study estimates that, globally, coastal assets at risk from a 100-year coastal flood will be some $35 trillion by 2070, up from $3 trillion in 2007. This more than tenfold increase does not bode well for the viability of future coastal economies around the world.

There is good news and bad about the capability of U.S. coastal states and communities to tackle these challenges in the future. The bad news is that most planners, engineers, and coastal officials are still in denial about the severity of the challenges and that relatively few state or local plans have taken sea level rise into account. To put an optimistic slant on the current state of affairs, coastal America is poised to begin to take on these difficult problems; and as the politics continues to change in favor of addressing climate change, it will become easier to make real progress.

The good news is that most Americans appear to believe that climate change is real, and a vast majority believe that actions to address climate change are needed. Other good news is that many of the steps and actions needed to move coastal jurisdictions toward greater resilience will also enhance long-term livability and quality of life in these places and can already be strongly justified on economic and environmental grounds. Conserving and restoring coastal ecosystems, for instance, will enhance resilience but will also yield many other benefits (e.g., biodiversity, recreation, tourism). Designing homes, schools, and offices so that they are survivable and livable in the aftermath of a hurricane means that they will also require less energy to operate, be less costly to heat and cool, and yield living and work environments (e.g., by incorporating natural daylight and natural ventilation) that are more enjoyable and productive. Strengthening social networks will make a community more resilient but will also result in richer human relationships, a stronger sense of community, and potentially greater meaning in life, all things that are intrinsically valuable. The agenda of resilient coastal communities need not be viewed as a bleak or burdensome one, but rather as a profoundly positive vision that holds great promise for improving the quality and experience of coastal living.

The resilience advocated here has many constituent elements and implies many different planning tools and policies. It suggests a profoundly new way of viewing coastal infrastructure—a new approach that values smaller, decentralized kinds of energy, water, and transport more suited to the dangerous physical conditions coastal communities will likely face. It suggests new ways of understanding community sustainability—arguing that sustaining, nurturing, and restoring coastal environments will be one of the essential planks in resilience, and that sustaining and nurturing a sense of community will be equally important. The new coastal resilience will require concerted work on the natural and built environments, and on the social, economic, and political ones as well.

What coastal resilience means in practice and on the ground is the main topic of this book. The other positive news is that there are now a number of hopeful stories, successful coastal planning and management cases, and a variety of tested tools and techniques for addressing the challenges faced. Coastal resilience will in practice likely require a creative mix of many different approaches: shoreline retreat and land use planning, greenhouse gas mitigation actions, and adaptations to climate change. As this book describes, there will be other strategies besides the obvious ones related to planning and physical design. In part, the task will involve ensuring that neighborhoods and communities prepare for and organize around these new threats, and that there are institutions and social capital to permit patterns of sharing, helping, and cooperation. The task will largely be about how to facilitate and grow resilient communities and neighborhoods and how to foster patterns of helpful relationships and interpersonal commitments.

The coastal management challenges we face in the next century and beyond are indeed daunting. Effective coastal management and planning responses to climate change and sea level rise will not occur quickly; they will likely be costly, entail significant buy-in from many different community interests, and require substantial lead time. And, as this book argues, effective responses will require some new ways of thinking and new ways of looking at the issues involved.

SECTION I:
COASTAL RESILIENCE:
BACKGROUND AND VULNERABILITY

CHAPTER 1

Coastal Resilience: What Is It?

THE CONCEPT OF *RESILIENCE* has emerged in the last decade as an important new way of thinking about the design and planning of coastal communities and regions. C. S. Holling's work on ecological resilience, beginning in the early 1970s, is often identified as the beginning point of discussions about resilience and its application to natural and social systems. Holling (1973, 9) speaks of the resilience of ecosystems as "the capacity of a system to absorb and utilize or even benefit from perturbations and changes that attain it, and so persist without a qualitative change in the system's structure."

The word *resilience* derives from the Latin *resiliere*, "to jump back" or "rebound," and in common usage refers to the ability to easily or quickly bounce back from a disturbance or crisis (Paton 2006). More specifically, when speaking of *resilience* in relation to coastal regions and communities, the themes of *flexibility*, *adaptability*, and *durability* are prominent in recent planning and management literature.

Resilience is further defined in the literature as

> the measure of how quickly a system recovers from failures (Emergency Management Australia 1998, as quoted in Buckle 2006, 90)

> the capacity to draw upon personal and social resources to manage the consequences of disasters (Paton, McClure, and Bürgelt 2006, 106)

> the ability of a community to not only deal with adversity but in doing so reach a higher level of functioning (J. Kulig, as cited in Pooley, Cohen, and O'Connor 2006, 163)

the potential of a system to remain in a particular configuration and to maintain its feedbacks and functions, and [involving] the ability of the system to reorganize following disturbance-driven change (Walker et al. 2002)

Berke and Campanella (2006, 193) define resiliency in the context of natural disasters as follows:

Achieving resiliency in a disaster context means the ability to survive future natural disasters with minimum loss of life and property, as well as the ability to create a greater sense of place among residents; a stronger, more diverse economy; and a more economically integrated and diverse population.

And, as Godschalk (2003) notes:

A resilient community is one that lives in harmony with nature's varying cycles and process. (p. 137)

Godschalk argues compellingly for a vision of resilient *cities*, and that resilience should be the "overriding goal" of urban hazard mitigation (italics mine):

Such cities would be *capable of withstanding severe shock* without either immediate chaos or permanent harm. Designed in advance to *anticipate, weather, and recover* from the impacts of natural or terrorist hazards, resilient cities would be built on principles derived from past experience with disasters in urban areas. While they might *bend from hazard forces, they would not break*. Composed of *networked social communities and lifeline systems, resilient cities would become stronger by adapting to and learning from disasters.* (pp. 136–37)

He continues:

Resilient cities are constructed to be *strong and flexible*, rather than brittle and fragile. Their lifeline systems of roads, utilities, and other support facilities are designed *to continue functioning in the face of rising water, high winds, shaking ground,* and terrorist attacks. Their new development is *guided away from known high hazard areas,* and their vulnerable existing development is relocated to safe areas. Their buildings are constructed or retrofitted to meet code standards based on hazard threats. Their natural *environmental protective systems* are conserved to maintain valuable hazard mitigation functions. Finally, their *governmental, non-governmental, and private sector organizations are prepared with up-to-date information about hazard vulnerability* and disaster resources, as linked with *effective communication networks,* and are experienced in working together. (p.137)

Resilience is often viewed as an antidote to vulnerability. Resilient communities work to reduce or even eliminate vulnerability. Vulnerability might be defined

4

"as the conditions determined by physical, social, economic, and environmental factors or processes, which increase the susceptibility of a community to loss from hazard impacts" (UN International Strategy for Disaster Reduction, as quoted in Buckle 2006, 90). Greater detail on the ways in which coastal communities and regions *are* vulnerable is provided in subsequent chapters of this book.

The notion of *adaptive capacity*—the idea that it is not simply possible or even desirable to return to a former condition; that entities (people, organizations, communities) should strive to learn from and creatively respond to disasters and disruptive events and trends; and that they should evolve and move from a crisis or disaster to a new and perhaps improved (but undoubtedly different) set of circumstances—is often a key feature in definitions of resilience. Resilience, then, according to Paton (2006, 8), is "a measure of how well people and societies can adapt to a changed reality and capitalize on the new possibilities offered." Recent coastal disaster events, such as Hurricane Katrina (see fig. 1.1), show compellingly the need to be ready to adapt to, and take advantage of, changed conditions and circumstances.

FIGURE 1.1

Hurricane Katrina resulted in more than $80 billion in property damages, the nation's most expensive hurricane, and demonstrated the extent to which urban populations in coastal cities like New Orleans are vulnerable. *Photo by Timothy Beatley.*

5

Implicit in the notion of resilience is an emphasis on taking actions and steps to build the adaptive capacity, to be ready ahead of a crisis or disaster. Resilience is *anticipatory*, *conscious*, and *intentional* in its outlook; while much cannot be known about future events, much can be anticipated, and planning ahead becomes a key aspect of resilience.

Resilience and Hazard Mitigation

Hazard mitigation has for several decades been the term within the natural hazards community for describing long-term anticipatory planning. More specifically, *hazard mitigation* refers to all the actions, steps, programs, and policies that can be adopted today to reduce loss of life and property damage in the event of a natural disaster (Godschalk et al. 1999).

Mitigation is often contrasted with preparedness and response activities. The focus in mitigation is on long-term, proactive steps (such as adopting and implementing building codes or construction standards, or prohibiting building in a high-risk coastal hazard zone), whereas preparedness and response actions are usually aimed at addressing fairly immediate health and safety concerns. Preparedness activities are those short-term actions undertaken immediately in advance of a natural disaster (e.g., evacuation in the face of an approaching hurricane); response activities are those actions taken immediately following an event (e.g., search and rescue, debris removal).

Planning for natural hazards is often conceptualized as occurring in four stages: (1) predisaster mitigation, (2) preparedness, (3) response, and (4) long-term recovery (fig. 1.2). Mitigation is viewed as possible, and as an essential goal, in the first and fourth of these stages. Many mitigative opportunities often emerge after a disaster event during the months and years of recovery. For example, it may be possible (and politically feasible) to put into place new development restrictions or stronger building standards after a large coastal storm; or there may be opportunities to relocate buildings and lifelines and to redesign infrastructure in ways that make them less vulnerable to the next disaster.

To a considerable extent, then, *resilience* has become the new way of talking about and advocating long-term mitigation. Resilience, however, differs from mitigation in at least two aspects: its focus on creative *adaptation* and learning and its focus on developing an underlying *capacity*.

While, historically, mitigation has meant physical changes (e.g., stronger build-

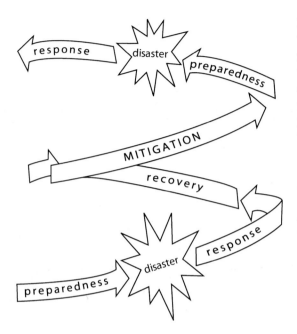

FIGURE 1.2
The four stages of disaster management. Opportunities to reduce long-term damages and to enhance coastal resilience are especially promising in the predisaster mitigation and postdisaster recovery and reconstruction stages. *Adapted from Godschalk, Brower, and Beatley,* Catastrophic Coastal Storms: Natural Hazard Mitigation and Development Management. *Copyright 1989, Duke University Press. Reprinted by permission of the publisher.*

ings), resilience is broader, connoting stronger social and community systems, and larger processes and mechanisms for facilitating effective response and recovery. There are certainly many physical design and building responses—for instance, elevating structures in the floodplain, or setting buildings back in areas subject to sea level rise—but community resilience must also be about developing supportive community institutions and networks that will help families and individuals to prepare for and respond to disaster events.

A philosophy of *disaster resistance*, on the other hand, implies a belief in our ability to armor or shield coastal communities and residents against the forces of nature. Seawalls, revetments, groins, jetties, and other shore-hardening structures reflect a disaster resistance approach; and beach renourishment, while a softer engineering strategy, still reflects an approach of resistance.

While structural shore hardening may be appropriate in some coastal circumstances, it is usually very costly and environmentally damaging, and it often offers a false sense of security or safety. For example, the 17-foot (5.2-meter) seawall at Galveston Island, Texas, only protects against a category 3 hurricane (for a complete explanation of the hurricane ranking system, see www.nhc.noaa.gov/aboutsshs.shtml). As Burby (2006) documents well, over the years, levee construction in New Orleans has led to massive urbanization in risky locations and, paradoxically, more people and property in harm's way.

What is needed in shifting coastal communities toward resilience is not just new politics, new tools, and new programs; underpinning these approaches must be a new way of looking at coastal change, a new way of thinking—what Walker and Salt (2006, 32) call *resilience thinking*—a way of thinking that acknowledges the fact that we're embedded in interconnected "socio-ecological systems," that these systems are complex and adaptive, and that resilience is "the capacity to undergo some changes without crossing a threshold to a different system regime." *Regime* here means a particular state or set of conditions that provide important values and benefits.

Resilience, as Walker and Salt effectively argue, addresses the social and economic as well as the ecological and finds application to many resource management issues:

> A resilient social-ecological system in a "desirable" state (such as a productive agricultural or industrial region) has a greater capacity to continue providing us with the goods and services that support our quality of life while being subjected to a variety of shocks. (p. 32)

> It's all about seeing a farm/family/business region as a complex adaptive system that's constantly changing and adapting to a changing world. (p. 113)

> Resilience is the capacity of this system to absorb change and disturbances, and still retain its basic structure and function—its identity. Resilience thinking is about envisaging a system in relation to thresholds. Is it approaching a threshold beyond which it will be in a new regime? What forces—economic, social and environmental—are driving the system toward this threshold? (p. 43)

Qualities of a Resilient Coastal Community

Walker and Salt (2006, 146) identify nine qualities or values that characterize a "resilient world" (box 1.1). While perhaps not all are immediately relevant to coastal hazards, they are useful to keep in mind. Resilience is characterized by *diversity* (biological, landscape, social, and economic) and by *ecological variability* (i.e., allowing ecosystems to change and move and "probe their boundaries"). A resilient world reflects a degree of *modularity* so that shocks and perturbations are controlled or contained. *Slow, controlling variables* receive emphasis in a resilient world; these are the ecological conditions or processes that help to control or stabilize change, such as the density of a key predator, or the nitrogen level in the soil, or the frequency of hurricanes. *Tight feedbacks* (i.e., how quickly and strongly the impacts of a change are felt) are an important quality in resilience, because they allow us to take actions and response steps before ecological and other thresholds are crossed (e.g., learning early that loss of coastal wetlands results in increasing coastal flooding might permit timely actions to prevent future losses).

A high degree of *social capital* is also viewed by Walker and Salt (2006, 47) as a very positive factor in promoting resilience:

> Resilience in social-ecological systems is very strongly connected to the capacity of the people in that system to respond, together and effectively, to change any disturbance. Trust, strong networks, and leadership are all important factors in making sure this can happen.

Innovation (placing "an emphasis on learning, experimentation, locally developed rules, and embracing change" [p.147]); *overlap in governance* (redundancy in governance structures); and, finally, *ecosystem services* (including the otherwise unpriced services provided by nature in our policy and planning deliberation) round out Walker and Salt's key values in a resilient world.

Resilience in coastal environments, indeed in all environments, can be understood as occurring at

---

Box 1.1 Qualities of a Resilient World

Some of the main qualities of a resilient world, according to Brian Walker and David Salt, include

1. *Diversity*
   A resilient world would promote and sustain diversity in all forms (biological, landscape, social, and economic).

2. *Ecological variability*
   A resilient world would embrace and work with ecological variability (rather than attempting to control and reduce it).

3. *Modularity*
   A resilient world would consist of modular components.

4. *Acknowledging slow variables*
   A resilient world would have a policy focus on "slow," controlling variables associated with thresholds.

5. *Tight feedbacks*
   A resilient world would possess tight feedbacks (but not too tight).

6. *Social capital*
   A resilient world would promote trust, well-developed social networks, and leadership (adaptability).

7. *Innovation*
   A resilient world would place an emphasis on learning, experimentation, locally developed rules, and embracing change.

8. *Overlap in governance*
   A resilient world would have institutions that include "redundancy" in their governance structures and a mix of common and private property with overlapping access rights.

9. *Ecosystem services*
   A resilient world would include all the unpriced ecosystem services in development proposals and assessments.

Source: Walker and Salt (2006).

multiple geographical scales. Resilience can apply at an individual or family level, but also at larger social or societal levels. Coastal resilience can best be viewed as a nested framework that understands that individual and family resilience are both constrained by and influenced by large societal and environmental settings, but that the latter are in turn affected by resilience, or the lack thereof, at smaller scales.

Resilience can be seen to exist, and can be nurtured, at both an individual and a collective level, and at a number of geographical scales (from neighborhood to region and beyond). Buckle (2006, 96) identifies certain elements that support resilience at an individual level, such as information and advice, resources (including financial), management capacity, personal and community support, and involvement. At the community level, Buckle (2006, 97–98) identifies the following as elements supporting resilience: knowledge of hazards; shared community values; established social infrastructure (e.g., information channels, social networks, and community organizations such as churches and supporting clubs); positive social and economic trends (e.g., a viable economy, a stable or growing population); partnerships; and resources and skills.

The resilience of a community can be viewed in terms of the resilience of its physical and built environments—the ability of a coastal community's homes and buildings and built infrastructure to withstand and adapt to natural forces and changing circumstances—and also in terms of the resilience of ecosystems and the natural environment. Will homes sustain wind forces? Are buildings and urban form sited away from and outside floodplains and high-risk locations and thus able to respond well to future flood events? Are the region's ecosystems and natural systems sufficiently intact and healthy that they will be equally resilient? Much more is presented later in this book about what resilient coastal growth and development patterns look like (see, especially, chapter 7).

A community's resilience can also be understood as a function of its social systems and networks and its levels of social and community support. Personal and community support include, according to Buckle (2006, 96), "post event personal support, such as outreach services, advocates and gatekeepers and community support, for example community development officers." Buckle uses the term *involvement* to indicate the broad importance of social networks and relationships. "Involvement" includes, according to Buckle (2006, 96), "linkages with other people, with a wide network of family, friends, and acquaintances shown to be critical in supporting and sustaining resilience." Paton (2006a, 309) puts forth a model of "comprehensive adaptive capacity" that views resilience as a function of two interacting realms:

(a) the individual (e.g. self-efficacy, sense of community, sense of place), community (e.g. reciprocal social support, collective efficacy, and societal/institutional (e.g. business continuity planning) resources required to support adaptation, and (b) the mechanisms that facilitate interaction within and between levels (e.g. social justice, community competence, trust, empowerment) in ways that promote cohesive action to enhance adaptive capacity, minimize disruption, and facilitate growth.

Paton (2006a, 308) presents vulnerability and resilience as opposing concepts, together determining risk in a community. "It is the relative balance of the vulnerability and resilience factors available or mobilized when confronting hazard effects that determine risk." He identifies the important dimensions of vulnerability and resilience at individual, community, and institutional/environmental levels and believes that, consistent with earlier definitions of resilience, disaster events or community perturbations can actually be opportunities to learn, adapt, and grow.

Paton (2006a, 315) advocates a community-based, bottom-up approach to resilience: "Resilience is about nurturing and sustaining the capacity of people, communities, and societal institutions to adapt to and experience benefit from disaster."

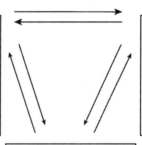

Sustainability
Protecting natural capital and assets of a community and region; taking action to reduce ecological footprint while enhancing health and quality of life in a community and region.

Hazard Mitigation
Steps to reduce exposure and vulnerability to natural assets; long-term actions to reduce extent of damage and impact from anticipated natural events.

Community Resilience
Ability of a community or region to adapt to and respond to disruptions and events of various sorts, including natural disasters.

FIGURE 1.3
Three interrelated concepts. Sustainability, mitigation, and resilience are interactive and reinforcing. For example, efforts at making a coastal community more sustainable can also enhance resilience, while steps to mitigate coastal hazards will enhance resilience and sustainability.

Advancing true resilience in coastal communities will require more than just a single or a handful of mitigative projects or actions. Rather, resilience requires thinking holistically, and taking many steps to *grow* a coastal culture and coastal societies that are resilient.

Resilience and Sustainability

Resilience and sustainability are highly related concepts; indeed, the former is often viewed as a foundation or "cornerstone" of the latter (fig. 1.3). The sustainability of an ecosystem, a landscape, or a city *requires* resilience. Resilience in and of itself is not intrinsically desirable—for example, maintaining or enhancing the resilience of a depleted resource (a fishery or a forest) is not a worthy goal. On the other hand, enhancing the resilience of a desired ecological or built form—for example a diverse ecosystem providing valuable benefits and services; a city or community providing a high quality of life; buildings and urban form providing shelter, jobs, and income— *is* a desirable and appropriate goal. In other words, the value of the regime or system we're attempting to make more resilient should be taken into account.

CHAPTER 2

The Vulnerability of Coastal Communities

COASTAL COMMUNITIES AND POPULATIONS face an extensive set of threats and hazards, including hurricanes, sea level rise, and earthquakes, among others (table 2.1). This chapter provides an extensive and detailed review of these threats, with particular focus on natural hazards, and seeks to establish a baseline understanding of the threats that coastal communities and regions are currently experiencing and will likely experience in the future. Subsequent chapters will identify the actions that coastal communities could take before and after natural disaster events, and the programs, policies, and projects that can help to make a community more resilient in the face of these threats.

There are a number of key drivers of unsustainable coastal development. These include coastal population growth, larger demographic trends, a desire to be near to and enjoy the amenities of coastal living, and a public policy and financial system that has largely encouraged and underwritten coastal risks. A limited understanding of the long-term (or even short-term) risks and dangers of living in coastal environments further contributes to these vulnerable patterns of development, as does a failure to adequately price and value natural ecosystems and ecosystem services.

High population and development growth rates in many coastal communities have led directly to degradation of the local and regional ecosystems that often provide resilience to those communities. What follows is a more detailed discussion of these drivers and the extent to which, and ways in which, coastal communities are vulnerable.

Table 2.1 Coastal Natural Hazards

CATEGORY	EVENT	HAZARDS
Meteorological	Nor'easters	Storm surges, high winds, heavy rain, flooding, possible heavy snows, coastal erosion
	Blizzards	Snow and freezing conditions, low visibility, damage to infrastructure, high winds
	Ice storms	Freezing conditions, damage to infrastructure, severe transportation disruption
	Hurricanes, tropical cyclones	Storm surge, high winds, possibility of tornadoes, heavy rain, flooding, coastal erosion
	Tornadoes	Extremely high winds, heavy rains, possible hail
	Drought and heat waves	Extreme temperatures, loss of crops, possible infrastructure damage
	Lightning	Electrical discharge, possibility of wildfires
	Hail	Often accompanies tornadoes; possibility of acute and extensive property damage
Geological	Earthquakes	Shaking terrain, possible ground rupture, landslides, destruction of homes and infrastructure
	Landslides and mudflows	Possibility of rockfalls, land subsidence, tsunamis, ground cracking
	Volcanoes	Lava flows, volcanic gases and aerosols, ground cracking, landslides, tsunamis
	Tsunamis	Massive storm surges, flooding, high potential for loss of property and life
Hydrological	Flood events	Erosion, landslides, increase in water levels, groundwater pollution
	El Niño, La Niña	Drought, flooding, frost, landslides, erratic temperatures and weather
	Wildfires	Result of natural or criminal causes and/or negligence; high possibility for great ecological, human, and property loss

Source: Table prepared by Javier De Castillo, Department of Urban and Environmental Planning, University of Virginia. Modified from Gregg and Houghton 2006.

Population Growth and Development

When one looks at the disproportionate tilt of population toward coastal regions, it can be said that the United States is a coastal nation. According to Crossett et al. (2004), while coastal counties, as defined by the National Oceanic and Atmospheric Administration (NOAA), make up only 17 percent of the nation's land area, they are home to more than 50 percent of its population; thus some of the highest urban densities are found in coastal areas. Twenty-three of the nation's twenty-five most densely populated counties and ten of the nation's most populous cites (including New York City) are found in coastal areas. Population growth is a major driver in U.S. coastal areas, and a major factor in determining the resilience of communities and regions. Between 1980 and 2003, coastal counties grew by a whopping 33 million people, or 28 percent. In the Southeast in particular, the rate of increase has been even more dramatic—almost 60 percent between 1980 and 2003. For a number of specific coastal states, the percentage of growth during this time was equally high or higher. Florida's population growth rose by an astounding 75 percent during this period. And while not growing at a faster rate, coastal areas are growing substantially as the nation's overall population grows (with coastal counties projected to add another 7 million people between 2003 and 2008).

This population growth translates into significant and often haphazard development pressures. As Crossett et al. (2004) report, nearly 3 million building permits were issued for single-family homes in coastal counties between 1999 and 2003, plus 1 million permits for multifamily homes. Much of this coastal development occurs in the form of *sprawl*, or what Richard Moe, president of the National Trust for Historic Preservation, defines as "low-density development at the edge of cities and towns, poorly planned, land-consumptive, auto-dependent, and designed without respect for its surroundings" (Moe 1994). This pattern of development is highly land-consumptive and destructive of natural features, and much of it is in areas subject to coastal hazards. Coastal seasonal or second homes are also a major driver, and more than half of the nation's stock of second homes was located in coastal counties (2.1 million) (NOAA n.d.).

In turn, economic drivers here include demand for second homes by baby boomers, and the economic and recreational pull of beaches and shorelines. Economic incentives that encourage and underwrite building construction in coastal areas include the ability to deduct mortgage interest and property taxes from federal income tax, and the gradual collectivizing of the private risks associated with buying and selling coastal property (e.g., federally subsidized flood insurance, damage loss deduction under the IRS code, federal disaster assistance). The view of real estate as an engine for personal investment and wealth generation, something uniquely American, is another factor that has stimulated growth and led to increasingly larger homes.

The Charleston, South Carolina, region is a good example of this pattern. From 1973 to 1994, for instance, the urbanized area reportedly grew by 256 percent, while the region's population grew by only 41 percent Allen and Lu (2003). Allen and Lu have undertaken a modeling exercise to attempt to predict what the Charleston region will likely look like in 2030. The results show that between 1994 and 2030, the size of the urbanized area will have grown from 250 square miles (ca. 647 square kilometers) to a whopping 868 square miles (2,248 square kilometers). These figures represent an almost 250 percent increase, compared with a nearly 50 percent increase in population (no small number in itself, of course). As a result, population density between 1994 and 2030 will have been reduced from more than 2,000 persons per square mile (per 2.6 square kilometers) to 917 persons per square mile. Most of the future growth will follow predictable patterns, spreading out along the shoreline and landward along highways and major transportation corridors.

This type of sprawling coastal land use pattern results in significant environmental damage and landscape alteration: loss of farmland and rural land; replacement of open and natural land with roads, parking lots, and impervious surfaces; and loss of wetlands and natural areas that help to buffer and protect the region from flooding and storms.

Physical Vulnerability

It is perhaps most logical to begin with a review of the geophysical forces and dynamics that exist in coastal areas that give rise to hazards and disaster vulnerability for coastal populations. By themselves these physical forces are benign and often beneficial. Hurricanes are a normal and ever-present aspect, for example, of coastal environments and actually perform critical environmental services, including the redistribution of energy and water and the renourishing of coastal ecosystems. Wildfires similarly serve positive ecological ends. The "hazard" or "vulnerability" arises *only after humans have placed themselves and their homes and property in harm's way.* Vulnerability, then, is generally a function of *the interaction of geophysical processes and forces and human decisions.*

Vulnerability is complicated somewhat by the likely anthropogenic dimensions of coastal forces (have hurricanes intensified as a result of human-induced global climate change?), but a healthy respect for and acknowledgment of the intrinsic riskiness of coastal environments and the need to design and plan and live with them in mind are a good place to start .

It is crucial to observe that coastal vulnerability is significantly influenced by the decisions individuals make (whether to build or buy a house in a particular location, whether or not to invest in mitigation measures) and the many planning and development decisions made by coastal localities. Both sets of decisions are commonly made without much regard for the long-term exposure and vulnerability to coastal hazards that result. In addition, there is inherent uncertainty about when events will occur: How fast will sea level rise occur and over what time frame? When will the next major hurricane strike? And when and how frequently will damaging seismic events occur?

Hurricanes, Nor'easters, Coastal Storms

The Atlantic and Gulf coasts are subject to intense and damaging storm activity, including hurricanes and tropical storms, as well as nor'easters. Since 1995, the United States has experienced a period of increased frequency and intensity of tropical storms (about fourteen per year, compared with an average of ten per year between 1850 and 1990; Pielke 2007).

Pielke et al. (2008) have "normalized" past hurricane activity (1900–2005) to give an estimate of what economic damage would have occurred under current patterns of population and economic exposure. The 1926 Great Miami Hurricane remains the most damaging, with $140–$157 billion (in 2005 dollars) in likely damages. As population growth in coastal areas continues, the potential for even larger economic loss increases. According to Pielke et al. (p. 38), "a simple extrapolation of the current trend of doubling losses every 10 years suggests that a storm like the 1926 Great Miami hurricane could result in perhaps $500 billion in damage as soon as the 2020s."

The work and analysis of Pielke and his colleagues should provide a cautionary warning for policy makers. As they conclude, the coastal U.S. faces a major challenge in moderating storm damages:

> Potential damage from storms is growing at a rate which may place severe burdens on society. Avoiding huge losses will require either a change in the rate of population growth in coastal areas, major improvements in construction standards, or other mitigation actions. Unless such action is taken to address the growing concentration of people and properties in coastal areas where hurricanes strike, damage will increase, and by a great deal, as more and wealthier people increasingly inhabit these coastal locations. (Pielke et al. 2008, 38).

Pielke (2007) further concludes that when future increases in the U.S. coastal population and its wealth, and even modest climate-change-induced increases in storm intensity, are taken into account, startling damage projections result.

There is growing consensus among climate scientists, moreover, that global climate change will result in stronger and more frequent hurricanes and coastal storms. Kevin Trenberth of the National Center for Atmospheric Research (NCAR) argues that evidence is convincing that as sea surface temperatures (SSTs) have risen, the number of larger hurricanes and storms has risen as well. Since the 1970s, SSTs have seen an increase of about 0.06 degree Celsius (ca. 0.11 degree Fahrenheit), and, as witnessed in the case of Hurricane Katrina, even a rise of 1 degree Celsius (1.8 degrees Fahrenheit) in SST can shift a hurricane an entire Saffir-Simpson intensity category (for a complete explanation of the hurricane ranking system, see www.nhc.noaa. gov/aboutsshs.shtml). Increasing SSTs are also believed to increase the rainfall associated with storms. As Trenberth (2007, 45), among others, concludes, global warming "clearly influences cyclone power and precipitation."

The Fourth Assessment Report of the Intergovernmental Panel on Climate Change (IPCC 2007a, 8) also concludes that such a link between climate change and increased North Atlantic hurricane activity is "more likely than not." Although this link is still controversial, many scientists believe hurricane intensity will further increase in the future. The IPCC Technical Summary (IPCC, 2007b, 174) concludes that model results indicate "a warmer future climate, increased peak wind intensities and increased mean and peak precipitation intensities in future tropical cyclones, with the possibility of a decrease in the number of relatively weak hurricanes, and increased numbers of intense hurricanes."

Other recent studies further buttress the prediction that hurricanes will grow in intensity, and that the numbers of intense storms will increase, as ocean waters warm. Researchers at Florida State University, for instance, have concluded that, as measured by wind speeds, hurricanes have already been intensifying (FSU 2008; see also Kerry 2005a, 2005b).

Sea Level Rise and Climate Change

Much of the U.S. coastline is highly vulnerable to even small amounts of sea level rise. Titus and Richmond (2001) estimate that around 60,000 square kilometers (23,166 square miles) along the Gulf and Atlantic coasts are at an elevation of 1.5 meters (ca. 5 feet) or less above sea level, with Florida, Louisiana, North Carolina, and Texas the most vulnerable.

If greenhouse gas (GHG) emissions continue over the next fifty years at current rates (often described as the business-as-usual scenario), global temperatures will likely rise by 5 degrees Fahrenheit (2.8 degrees Celsius) by the end of the century. Jim Hansen (2006), director of the National Aeronautics and Space Administration's Goddard Institute for Space Studies, notes that the last time the Earth experienced temperatures that high was 3 million years ago, and sea levels then were 82 feet (25 meters) higher than today. Similarly high sea levels would inundate large portions of the United States, areas inhabited by 50 million Americans, though it might take several centuries for sea level to reach this height. Hansen (2006) says, "In that case, the United States would lose most East Coast cities: Boston, New York, Philadelphia, Washington, and Miami; indeed, practically the entire state of Florida would be under water." Significant melting of ice sheets already appears to be happening. A dramatic expansion of the areas of the Greenland Ice Sheet experiencing summer melting (an increase of 50 percent in the last twenty-five years), a marked increase in the volume of icebergs , and what Hansen calls a "shocking" increase in "icequakes" (caused by ice sheet movements) are all disturbing signs.

Paleoclimatic evidence suggests that, assuming a continuing rise in GHG emissions, long-term sea level rise (after 2100), could be even more dramatic. Jonathan Overpeck and his colleagues have analyzed the last major warming of the Earth (about 130,000 years ago) and concluded that similar sea level rises (4 to >6 meters, or ca. 13 to >19 feet) are possible, but with levels rising more rapidly than commonly thought (Overpeck et al. 2006). Overpeck and Jeremy Weiss have generated maps at the University of Arizona Environmental Studies Laboratory that show visually, and in dramatic fashion, what a 6-meter (19.7-foot) rise in sea level would actually mean for the Atlantic and Gulf coasts (their maps can be found at www.geo.arizona.edu/dgesl).

Sea level rise is not a theoretical possibility but rather has been occurring throughout the last century, with acceleration over the last decade (about 1.2 inches [ca 3 centimeters] over these ten years; see Dean 2006). Sea levels rise primarily as a result of thermal expansion and mass inputs of freshwater as a result of melting ice sheets (the latter increasingly understood to be the more significant contributor as glacial melting has accelerated). The Fourth Assessment Report of the IPCC (2007a, 7) predicts that, globally, sea levels will rise from 0.6 to 1.9 feet (0.18–0.58 meter) by the end of the close of the twenty-first century. Some believe the IPCC estimate to be conservative (not fully taking into account mass inputs of freshwater). And even the IPCC report admits that with the possibility of the complete melting of the Antarctic and Greenland ice sheets, sea levels could reach much higher levels.

Shown in figure 2.1 are portions of New York City that will likely flood during a category 3 hurricane under different sea level rise scenarios. As the large areas of blue indicate, assuming sea level rise continues at current rates, large areas of the city will by 2050 be vulnerable to extensive flooding from even modest hurricane events.

Cynthia Rosenzweig and her colleagues (Columbia University, n.d.; Jacob, Gornitz, and Rosenzweig 2007) at the Goddard Institute for Space Studies have been analyzing the extent to which the New York City metropolitan area would be vulnerable to sea level rise and storms. With a shoreline of some 2,400 kilometers (ca. 1,500 miles), and with much of its most critical infrastructure (airports, rail lines, highways) less than 3 meters (ca.10 feet) above sea level, rapid sea level rise would be disastrous for this city. Figure 2.1 shows graphically the extent of flooding that would result from a worst-case category 3 hurricane striking the city. Other coastal cities, and millions of urban residents, are equally vulnerable to such events in the future.

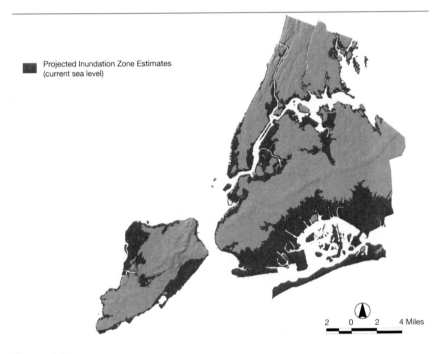

Projected Inundation Zone Estimates
(current sea level)

2   0   2   4 Miles

FIGURE 2.1
Projected New York City inundation zone estimates following a category 3 hurricane occurring at current sea level. Adapted from original image by New York City Department of Environmental Protection, Columbia University Center for Climate Systems Research, HydroQual, and State University of New York Stony Brook.

Earthquakes and Tsunamis

Much of the U.S. coastline falls within areas of significant seismic activity. Some of the more damaging earthquake events have struck coastal communities and cities, such as the 1886 earthquake that devastated Charleston, South Carolina. Many coastal population centers, including Boston in the Northeast, Seattle and Portland in the Northwest, and much of California, face serious seismic hazards. The existence of many unreinforced masonry buildings and areas where construction of bridges and other public infrastructure has not incorporated seismic design standards contributes to coastal vulnerability.

The December 2004 Sumatra earthquake and Indian Ocean tsunami have resulted in much new (and needed) awareness about the tsunami threat. Tsunamis are sea waves that are typically caused by offshore seismic events (and are often referred to as "seismic sea waves"). These waves radiate out from an offshore epicenter and can cause tremendous damage and loss of life in low-lying coastal areas. California's Seismic Safety Commission released an assessment in 2005 of the state's vulnerability to tsunamis, concluding that they "pose a significant threat to life and property" (California Seismic Safety Commission, 2005, 1) and pointing out the extent to which mitigation and preparedness are presently inadequate (e.g., seismic building code standards that don't really address the likely forces a tsunami will generate). In California, there have been 82 tsunami events observed or recorded over the last 150 years, several of which were very damaging, including a 21-foot (6.4-meter) wave length experienced in Crescent City during the 1964 tsunami. It is estimated that more than 1 million Californians live within tsunami-vulnerable coastal areas, as well as thousands of tourists and visitors (California Seismic Safety Commission, 2005, 5). California's seaports are seen to be particularly vulnerable to tsunami damages.

Drought, Heat Waves, Wildfires

Coastal communities also will experience higher-than-typical summer temperatures and face a need to adapt to heat wave and drought events. Barry Lynn and his colleagues at the NASA Goddard Institute for Space Studies predict significant increases in surface temperatures over the eastern United States as a result of climate change. By the 2080s, average daily high temperatures that today are in the low to mid-80s in degrees Fahrenheit (ca. 27–30 degrees Celsius) would rise to the low to mid-90s (ca. 32–35 degrees Celsius) and in late summer could rise to between 100 and 110 degrees Fahrenheit (ca. 38–43 degrees Celsius) (Druyan, Lynn, and

Healy 2007; Lynn, Healy, and Druyan 2007; NASA 2007). This increase is in addition to the hotter temperatures many urbanized coastal cities already experience through the urban heat island effect (New York City's summer nocturnal temperatures are already more than 7 degrees Fahrenheit (ca. 4 degrees Celsius) hotter than surrounding, less urbanized areas) (Rosenzweig et al. 2006).

Global warming will also likely exacerbate many other existing problems faced by coastal cities and regions. A recent study of 50 eastern U.S. cities by Bell et al. (2007, 61) predicts that urban concentrations of ozone will increase there by 2050, and that the greatest increases will occur in cities that already have the highest levels of ozone pollution. The number of days in which federal ozone standards are failed will increase, and respiratory and other associated health implications will be significant.

Coastal Resource Depletion

Coastal communities also face many other related natural resource constraints and limitations that often leave a community and region more susceptible to natural disasters when they strike. Many, perhaps most, coastal communities around the world face serious and long-term shortages of potable freshwater. A combination of profligate use and waste, water shortages are exacerbated by climate and drought, though the underlying causes may be more complex (a combination of high usage, population growth, and unsustainable sourcing). Similarly, a variety of other coastal resources—from forests and farmland and the timber, food and other goods and products generated from them, to fisheries—are now commonly in short supply and in decline. The decline may be gradual, but it often results in episodic crises. These forms of coastal resource decline in turn affect the economic resilience of a coastal community or region.

Social Vulnerability

Vulnerability is also a function of social and community variables. "Social vulnerability," as Cutter, Boruff, and Shirley (2003, 242) note, "varies over space and time," and will depend on an interaction of social, economic, and biophysical factors. Indicators of social vulnerability include age, income and poverty, housing stock, race, and the presence or absence of social networks and social support structures that could help in the event of a disaster. (For a more extensive review of social vulnerability variables see Cutter, Boruff, and Shirley 2003.)

Each of these demographic and social categories suggests special vulnerability in the face of coastal hazards and disaster events. Elderly residents with limited mobility may have difficulty, for instance, evacuating in advance of an oncoming storm. Those who are the poorest members of the community will have the fewest resources with which to prepare for or respond to an emergency or disaster event. In New Orleans during Hurricane Katrina, the absence of cars among the poorer residents, largely African Americans, resulted in special vulnerability, as these residents had difficulty evacuating before the storm, as well as escaping the city after it. Katrina also vividly demonstrated the implications of race. Cutter, Boruff, and Shirley (2003, 253) argue convincingly the importance of social and ethnic geography in explaining vulnerability. For African Americans in New Orleans, vulnerability is tied to a long history of segregation and disparities in opportunities and access to resources: "Race contributes to social vulnerability through the lack of access to resources, cultural differences, and the social, economic and political marginalization that is often associated with racial disparities." Other ethnic and demographic variables—for instance, having lived only shortly in the community, or an inability to speak English—may as a consequence result in serious impediments to preparing for and responding to a disaster event, and to accessing and taking advantage of disaster recovery services and benefits.

The quality and tenure of housing is perhaps an obvious determinant of vulnerability. Homes vary considerably in terms of their strength, design, and quality of construction. Mobile homes are typically more vulnerable because of their less substantial construction, their frequent lack of adequate anchoring, and their frequent siting in higher-risk locations. In coastal regions with a high seismic threat (e.g., California and the Northwest), unreinforced masonry buildings are especially dangerous. The tenure and ownership status is also relevant: renters, for instance, may have far fewer resources with which to rebound from a disaster event.

It is also clear that the degree of social isolation in a neighborhood or community will also influence vulnerability, and in this regard the overall trends in the United States are not encouraging. Recent evidence suggests that Americans exhibit an even greater degree of social isolation today than just two decades ago. McPherson, Smith-Lovin, and Bashears (2006, 353) found in their analysis of the 2004 General Social Survey that respondents indicated a decline (compared with 1995) in the number of people with whom they are able to discuss important matters.

Alarmingly, these researchers found a substantial drop in the extent to which Americans have discussion networks within their neighborhoods and communities (people in whom they can confide about life's ups and downs). The number of respondents indicating that they had no one to talk with has actually tripled in these two decades.

Social connectedness and networks of supportive friends and family are valuable conditions for social resilience, though they are sometimes overlooked. As McPherson, Smith-Lovin, and Bashears (2006, 354) indicate: "Social scientists know that contacts with other people are important in both instrumental and socioemotional domains. . . . The closer and stronger our tie with someone, the broader the scope of their support for us . . . and the greater the likelihood that they will provide major help in a crisis."

Economic Vulnerability

While individual income level can be an indicator of social vulnerability, the community's or region's economic base must also be robust and diverse enough to weather an economic downturn or global economic shock. In many coastal communities, economic vulnerability can be seen in the form of overreliance on one industry or industrial sector, or on one employer. This economic vulnerability has been experienced by some coastal regions in the form of overreliance on military facilities that then have been closed or relocated.

Cutter, Boruff, and Shirley (2003, 253) identify "single-sector economic dependence" as a significant variable in social vulnerability as well, so they are closely connected. In their words:

> A singular reliance on one economic sector for income generation creates a form of economic vulnerability for counties. The boom and bust economies of oil development, fishing, or tourism-based coastal areas are good examples— in the heyday of prosperity, income levels are high, but when the industry sees hard times or is affected by a natural hazard, the recovery may take longer.

As these authors note, heavy reliance also on the agricultural sector, in light of inherent vagaries of weather and price, is another form of economic vulnerability.

The case studies in section III demonstrate convincingly the importance of the health of a community's and region's economy to its overall resilience. Charleston, South Carolina, illustrates the difficulties associated with naval facility closures and provides a positive story of a community able to rebound and to promote a stronger, more resilient economy in the face of this economic blow.

As a further example, the negative impacts associated with Hurricane Katrina

24

and the difficult recovery there were strongly foreshadowed by a weak and struggling economy with high unemployment and low economic productivity. Weak coastal economies do not bode well for resilient responses and quick recoveries from a major hurricane. In turn, stronger social cohesion and stronger social networks and capital can work together to enhance resilience in the face of these economic conditions (and thus the social and economic variables are interconnected in some critical ways).

Economic resilience is a major aspect of disaster resilience in the sense that a resilient coastal community will require businesses to be able to quickly adapt, rebuild, and reopen. To this end, how many local businesses, how much of a community's economic sector, are situated in high-risk locations? How many businesses have prepared business continuity plans, and how many have generally taken steps to think ahead of time about the likely impacts of a future natural event? As well, what mechanisms—economic, social, and organizational—have been put in place by local governments to help businesses following a major disaster?

Declining Oil Supplies

Coastal communities face a number of other potentially severe shocks and disruptions that may be viewed as vulnerabilities and that, taken together with hazard and biophysical vulnerabilities, exacerbate these vulnerabilities.

American society and the U.S. economy are highly dependent on fossil fuels, oil in particular. Much discussion and writing has occurred in the last five years about the prospects of a sharp decline in oil supply. While not yet a consensus theory, peak oil theory argues that soon, likely within the next ten years, global oil production will peak, and will begin an inevitable downward decline. Rapidly rising oil prices, supply disruptions, and a general sharp decline in available supplies are major social and economic disruptions that coastal communities may need to anticipate and plan for (e.g., see Heinberg 2003). Good land use practices, for instance, encouraging mixed-use, walkable neighborhoods that rely less on automobiles for mobility, will yield more resilient communities in the face of declining oil supplies.

Coastal communities are vulnerable to this disruption and potentially rapid decline for several reasons, including the following:

- Car-dependent communities, lifestyles, and land use patterns
- Poor public transit systems
- Land use and growth patterns that provide few feasible alternatives to the

use of the car (walking and bicycling are difficult)

In what ways might coastal communities become more resilient in the face of diminishing oil resources? Here are a few:

- Create more compact growth patterns that are less dependent on car transport
- Plan for and expand options and alternatives to cars, including walking, bicycles, and public transit
- Move in the direction of more localized systems of production and consumption—for instance, strengthening local food production, processing, and distribution systems (e.g., farmers' markets, CSAs, and farm-to-school programs)
- Shift to local economies and economic developments that are less fossil-fuel and energy intensive

Ironically, in coastal areas where significant habitat and land restoration work is undertaken, which should make the region more resilient on many levels, this work is often very energy- and oil-intensive. Day et al. (2005, 261–62) argue that, in the future, much of this restoration work will need to occur through the harnessing of the natural powers of nature:

> If the end of era of cheap energy comes to pass, energy intensive management methods will become increasingly expensive and untenable. . . . We will be forced to consider less energy-intensive, less expensive options for restoring deteriorating coastal marshes in the post-oil peak era.
>
> Increased cost and reduced availability of energy suggests that those methods of restoration that use relatively low amounts of energy are the ones most sustainable in the long run.
>
> Wherever possible, gravity, winds, and tides should be used to move water and sediments. . . . Energy intensive approaches, such as pumping sediments over long distances to build wetlands, should be used now but they may not be affordable 40–50 years from now.

Many of the actions and steps that would help make coastal communities more resilient in the face of declining oil supplies will also address many of the other sustainable goals and challenges faced. Reducing auto dependence will actually mean cleaner air, less energy consumption, and fewer greenhouse gas emissions, thus helping to address global climate change.

Section II
Approaches to Planning
for Coastal Resilience

CHAPTER 3

Coastal Resilience: Key Planning Dimensions

SEVERAL PLANNING DIMENSIONS ARE KEY to advancing coastal resilience: resilience of land use and built form; resilience of ecosystems and natural coastal environments; social resilience; and economic resilience. These dimensions are obviously not mutually exclusive, but rather are interactive and interconnected. Changes in coastal land use patterns and urban form can serve to reduce direct exposure to natural hazards (by avoiding floodplains or high-erosion zones, for instance), but they may also help to promote social interaction and to build a sense of community, in turn enhancing social resilience. Actions to strengthen economic resilience may, as a further example, help ensure that companies can function and reopen quickly following a storm or natural event, thereby helping to buffer the individuals and families that depend on the jobs and income these companies provide. Limiting such business disruptions in coastal areas, then, helps to enhance social resilience. While it is certainly possible that actions taken to enhance resilience in one realm might work against resilience in another realm, most often, investments in resilience in one realm help to advance resilience in the other dimensions as well.

In this chapter we briefly introduce these key planning dimensions and discuss the types of measures and actions that might be aimed at enhancing or strengthening them. More detailed discussions of land use and built environment, and the specific tools and techniques that might be employed, can be found in chapter 7.

Resilience of Land Use and Built Environment

The vulnerability of a coastal community or region to a natural hazard such as an earthquake or hurricane often manifests in the clearest and most visceral way with respect to the built environment. Hurricane winds and surge inundation wreak havoc on buildings, streets, neighborhoods. Families return to find homes destroyed, infrastructure damaged or destroyed, roads impassable, and services and facilities disrupted. These impacts on the built environment suggest the clearest (though certainly not easy) set of actions and steps that communities and regions might take to reduce long-term damage and disruption and thus make the community more resilient.

What follows is a discussion of resilient land use, organized around three geographical groupings: the community and regional levels, the neighborhood and site level, and the building and facility level. Action at each geographical level is required. This multiscale design and planning framework is presented in box 3.1.

Community and Regional Land Use and Growth Patterns

Avoidance of natural hazards is perhaps the most effective coastal resilience strategy, one that can be effected by steering development away from high-risk locations, such as floodplains and seismic fault zones. Local and regional land acquisition efforts can be aimed at setting aside these most dangerous locations, and at trying to ensure a healthy coastal ecosystem that preserves the mitigative features of the natural environment. More specifically, coastal communities can

- prepare comprehensive plans or community land use plans that guide future growth away from and out of these risky locations;
- use land use regulatory tools, such as zoning, to keep the extent of density and development away from high-risk locations;
- impose performance standards to reduce exposure (for instance, by requiring new development to be set back a minimum distance from high-erosion shorelines);
- create hazard mitigation plans.

The many specific tools and techniques that can be employed in these efforts are discussed in greater detail in chapter 7.

It is critical as well, to work toward resilience at the broader geographical scale of the region or bioregion. While examples of effective regional planning are few in the United States, it is nevertheless useful to understand how an individual locality's efforts can fit within, complement, and be complemented by efforts in other localities and

Box 3.1 Planning for Coastal Resilience at Different Scales

SCALES	DESIGN AND PLANNING ACTIONS AND IDEAS
Building	Energy Star house
	Passive solar design
	Local materials
	Solar water heating/photovoltaic panels
	Safe room
	Rainwater collection/purification
	Passive survivability
	Green rooftops and rooftop gardens
	Daylit interior spaces and natural ventilation
Street	Green streets
	Urban trees
	Low-impact development (LID)
	Street designed for stormwater collection
	Vegetated swales and narrow streets
	Edible landscaping
	Pervious/permeable surfaces
	Sidewalks and walkable streets
Block	Green courtyards
	Setback from ocean or high-hazard area
	Clustered housing outside of floodplains and high-hazard areas
	Photovoltaics
	Native species yards and spaces
Neighborhood	Stream daylighting, stream restoration
	Decentralized/distributed power
	Urban forests
	Community gardens
	Neighborhood parks/kitchens, pocket parks
	Greening greyfields and brownfields
	Neighborhood grocery, food center, or co-op
	Neighborhood energy/disaster response councils/committees
Community	Urban creeks and riparian areas
	Urban ecological networks
	Walking, hiking, biking trails
	Green schools
	City tree canopy
	Community forest coverage (min 40%)/community orchards
	Greening utility corridors
	Disaster shelters and evacuation capacity
Region	Conservation of wetlands
	River systems/floodplains
	Riparian systems
	Regional greenspace systems
	Greening major transport corridors
	Regional evacuation capacity

Source: Modified from Girling and Kellett (2005, 58).

the region as a whole. Preserving regional systems of greenspace, protecting those essential elements of a green infrastructure network, and restoring regional ecosystem functions, for instance, are important strategies for enhancing resilience. Many aspects of resilience—from evacuation, to infrastructural investments of all kinds, to sustainable economic development—are best viewed through a regional lens.

Neighborhood and Site Level

Design and planning actions at the neighborhood or site level can enhance resilience in many ways. Neighborhoods can be designed and built with wind-resistant and flood-resistant trees and vegetation, and can incorporate a number of urban greening ideas and techniques, from rain gardens to green rooftops to permeable paving, that will enhance resilience. Many of these techniques and design strategies are discussed in greater detail in later chapters, and in the case studies of resilient coastal communities and projects.

Building and Facility Level

Complete avoidance of hazard areas is often not possible in many coastal areas. Buildings and homes throughout a coastal region must expect to experience and withstand the high winds associated with hurricanes and tropical storms, at least along the Atlantic and Gulf coasts of the United States. Building codes and coastal construction standards that address hazards are an essential aspect of coastal resilience.

Moreover, building construction is increasingly recognized as providing tremendous new opportunities to reduce our energy and ecological demands, and to enhance broader goals of resilience, such as less dependence on fossil fuels. "Passive survivability"—the idea that buildings should be designed to survive the loss of essential services in the event of a natural disaster—has become a new structural design goal since Hurricane Katrina, which made clear that homes must provide the conditions for safe living following a disaster (daylight, natural ventilation, on-site water collection, etc.). There are now a number of compelling examples of creative, sustainable, and safer buildings to point to and learn from, as well as a number of certification systems that are helpful in promoting sustainable and resilient building design (e.g., Leadership in Energy and Environmental Design, or LEED). Buildings can be designed ideally to withstand greater wind speeds and seismic shaking forces. They can be designed so as to utilize natural daylight, allow natural ventilation, and include power generation that does not rely on the coastal power grid (e.g., photovoltaic panels, solar hot water heating systems). Strategies for designing buildings for passive survivability and for resilience in the face of natural forces are described in greater detail in chapter 7.

Ecological Resilience

The ecosystems and natural environments of coastal regions are at once *subject to* perturbations and impacts of natural events such as hurricanes (and longer-term changes such as global climate change and sea level rise) and essential *moderators of* the impacts of these forces on people and built form. We can meaningfully speak, then, about both of these dimensions: the resilience of these ecosystems and natural systems in the face of perturbations, and the positive role they play in enhancing the resilience of built environments and human communities.

Examples of planning actions that might be taken to ensure the ecological resilience in the built environments and human communities include the following:

- Ensuring sufficient wetlands buffers
- Permitting coastal wetlands to migrate landward in response to long-term sea level rise
- Protecting ecological systems and land area (landscape) sufficiently large and complex and diverse that any particular perturbation (storm, wildfire) will not cause irreversible harm (e.g., extinction of a species, complete loss of a biological community)

Examples of planning for ecological resilience in the latter category might include ensuring the existence and health of beach and dune systems because they are effective flood barriers, or preserving extensive coastal marsh systems because they act as natural sponges, retaining large amounts of floodwaters. Indeed, many of the actions that could be taken to enhance ecological resilience of one type will help to advance the other.

Social Resilience in Coastal Communities

Coastal communities are not simply or primarily composed of buildings and infrastructure, but of people—individuals, families, and social groups of various sorts—and thus many resilience efforts must be aimed directly at them. How will individuals and families cope with and respond to crises and natural events, and what factors help to explain successful and effective coping? What individual and social resources exist to help in coping and rebounding? What social structures or institutions or programs might help individuals, families, and communities to better cope? There are strong reasons to think that coastal communities that have nurtured certain social qualities, conditions, and relationships will be more resilient in the face of natural disasters and other disruptions.

Box 3.2 presents the story of the recovery of the Vietnamese community of New Orleans' Versailles neighborhood following Hurricane Katrina. Here recovery has been highly successful on almost every measure, from quickly reopened stores to maintaining the prestorm population, aided by a strong social network, shared values, and social institutions, including the Catholic Church. Some critical lessons can be gleaned from recent coastal disaster events about the value of

---

Box 3.2 The Resilience of the Versailles Community in the Aftermath of Katrina

The Versailles neighborhood in eastern New Orleans, a community of Vietnamese immigrants, has recovered and rebounded from Hurricane Katrina in a remarkable way, and most residents have returned to the neighborhood (unlike in the rest of the city). Stores and restaurants reopened relatively quickly, and through a sense of shared mission, roofs have been replaced and homes repaired. Recovery in Versailles (also now known as Viet Village) has not waited for official government help or decisions, but proceeded when the residents of the neighborhood made a decision that the neighborhood would return and coordinated actions to bring this about. At the center of the shared mission was the Catholic Church—especially the Mary Queen of Vietnam Church and its active pastor, Vien Nguyen. The church actually sheltered many residents during the storm itself and has taken the role of catalyst and coordinator following the storm. The church's van helped transport residents, and permitted travel to other cities where residents had evacuated. In the face of no electricity, the community, again with the church coordinating, submitted a petition signed by 500 residents to Entergy, the local electric utility, with the result being restored electricity. More recently, the community mobilized itself to oppose the dumping of debris on a wetland site only about a mile away from Versailles. Residents worried about the possible pollution impacts of this unlined debris site and through demonstrations were eventually able to convince Mayor Nagin to close the site (and are now mobilizing to have the debris already dumped at the site taken away). The effort at tackling the debris landfill seems to confirm that the community stewardship ethic tends to flow from this kind of cultural and social attachment to place and community.

In Versailles, the hurricane is also being seen as a positive catalyst for strengthening and improving the community. A community development corporation (CDC—usually a nonprofit community-based organization aimed at improving housing and living conditions for those most in need) has been created, and there are big plans for the future including construction of a retirement community, a new charter school, a farmer's co-op and expanded farmers' market, and a large community garden adjacent to the church.

such social networks, resources, and institutions. The story of Versailles is one of a strong and cohesive community, with the Mary Queen of Vietnam Church and its active pastor serving as essential community anchors, coordinating and mobilizing that community's very successful recovery efforts.

Nurturing cohesive neighborhoods and helping to build stronger ties between neighbors will enhance the effectiveness of response and recovery following a coastal disaster. An image of neighbors in the suburbs of Washington, DC, grappling with the stinging aftermath of Hurricane Isabel in 2003 comes to mind. Many homes were without electricity for days, but others were not. At least some of the lucky families with power shared this limited resource by way of long extension cords

Box 3.2 Continued

What explains the success of the recovery of this community in the face of so much failure throughout New Orleans? While the neighborhood experienced significant damage (flooding as high as 4 meters, or about 13 feet, in places), this was much less than that incurred by many other areas of the city. Perhaps most important is the cultural cohesiveness and strong sense of community that exists. As Pastor Nguyen says, "Other people have neighborhoods, we have a community" (as quoted in Strange 2006). Retaining a strong common culture and heritage and religion are, of course, important elements in this strong sense of community. And the history of overcoming hardship has been an important factor as well. The Vietnamese residents here have endured before—in particular, several times having to migrate to avoid the expansion of the communism in Vietnam, first in the 1950s, then in 1975 with the fall of Saigon.

The important role of the Catholic Church cannot be overlooked as a key element of social cohesion, and a mechanism for communicating with residents and sharing resources and coordinating recovery activity. It made possible, moreover, a coordinated and clear decision to rebuild, minimizing the risk and uncertainty associated with individual decisions in most other neighborhoods in the city (should I rebuild if others will not?). The church, and Nguyen in particular, have served, in his words, as a "strong anchor" for the community. Along with this cohesiveness goes a cultural value system that acknowledges a strong sense of responsibility to the collective or community, quite at odds perhaps with the prevailing and excessive individualism that characterizes much of American society. One commentator (Hill 2006), writing in the *Louisiana Weekly*, described the importance of a "group-oriented culture" in explaining the "Miracle of Versailles," which

emphasized community needs over individual rights and interests; each individual in the community was duty-bound to help everyone in their community make it home. From the outset, community members understood that the individual's survival depended on the community's survival.

snaking their way across residential streets and sidewalks (e.g., Pearlstein and Argetsinger, 2003). In the aftermath of Hurricane Katrina in 2005, when the ability to cook food was limited (many damaged homes were left with no functioning kitchen), it was not uncommon for those who could cook to prepare meals for neighbors who could not. Cohesive neighborhoods, where individuals and families know and trust each other and where there is a willingness to help and share resources (food, labor, information, etc.) will contribute much to overall coastal resilience.

The extent of personal engagement and participation in a community is another important aspect of social resilience. Widespread public engagement and participation in the preparation of hazard mitigation plans has been shown to increase the effectiveness and successful implementation of these plans (Burby 2003). Berke and Campanella (2006, 203) are especially eloquent in arguing for participation and engagement as prerequisites for a resilient community and identifying a number of clear benefits from this participation: "The wider the range of participants, the greater the opportunity." They believe that citizen support for resilience will tend to bring public officials along: "When citizens start to grasp the more resilient and more sustainable alternatives for living with hazards, they mobilize and begin to insist that elected officials make decisions leading to long-term resiliency."

Facilitating that community involvement and engagement, and helping to build the civic skills and "renewed civic institutions" that will allow this to happen, are crucial steps on the way to coastal resilience. Social resilience, then, requires bolstering and strengthening social networks, and nurturing relationships between the organizations and institutions that already exist (e.g., Berke and Campanella 2006).

Box 3.3 Local Strategies for Strengthening and Expanding Social Capital

- Create neighborhood planning processes that engage citizens.
- Engage in community design that facilitates and encourages social interaction (e.g., compact, walkable neighborhoods, connected street and trail system, mixed uses with extensive civic realm).
- Invest in farmers' markets, neighborhood markets, community supported agriculture (CSAs).
- Support block parties and neighborhood street festivals.
- Support community clubs and associations.
- Support nature-based community learning (e.g., birdwatching clubs, fungi forays, astronomy clubs, star gazing parties).
- Undertake ecological restoration and community repair work.
- Establish new community spaces and gathering areas.
- Underwrite active community or neighborhood associations.

36

Some evidence also suggests that a sense of community, and of belonging to a community, many enhance adaptive response and adaptive capacity. "Sense of community and place attachment represent resources capable of contributing to the capacity of individuals and communities to cope with or adapt to environmental hazard impacts" (Paton, Kelly, and Doherty 2006, 204). Viewing oneself as part of a mutually interdependent community, and undertaking steps through which bonds and "emotional investments" can occur, may yield tremendous benefits in the form of community resilience. Influences on the formation of place bonds or place attachments are likely many, but active participation and engagement is one significant one, to be sure.

The potential resilience outcomes of these place attachments are many as well, and might be evident in some of the following ways: helping neighbors and sharing materials, food, and resources following a disaster; assisting neighbors in navigating the recovery process and sharing information about recovery programs; volunteering before and after a disaster event; returning to the community following an event, and committing to staying in that community even in the face of economic and population outmigration (see box 3.3). Such a sense of community, or commitment to community, can in potentially innumerable ways strengthen the community's social networks and shared value structure, upon which successful adaptive response can occur.

It should also be noted that a coastal community will generally be more resilient, the more emotionally (and physically) healthy its residents are. Contact with nature, for instance, is a significant stress reducer and provides substantial emotional and mental health benefits. A community that provides greater access to nature and natural systems will be more resilient by virtue of the health benefits provided. As Paton, Kelly. and Doherty (2006, 206) conclude:

> It is evident . . . that interaction with the environment can perform a restorative function and contribute to well-being. It can also act as a protective factor in regard to mitigating present and future stress, act as a catalyst for meaningful interaction that facilitates the development and/or maintenance of *adaptive competencies* (e.g., self- and collective efficacy), and contribute to the development and maintenance of attachment and commitment to place/community.

Additional work is required to identify how much environmental experience is sufficient, what qualities it should contain and whether different kinds of environmental engagement can be differentiated in regard to their restorative and protective capacity. . . . For example, to what extent is its restorative and adaptive capacity linked to passive (e.g., visiting a natural environment) versus active participation (e.g., ornithology, volunteering for land care projects). While passive interaction may still convey restorative benefits, it may lack the quality of meaningful interaction that underpins the development and maintenance of adaptive capacity (i.e., that facilitate the sense of challenge that contributes to environmental experience enhancing self-efficacy) or that contribute to a sense of place attachment. In the absence of the latter, the quality of adaptive capacity may be diminished.

Economic Resilience

A strong argument can be made that one of the most effective approaches to enhancing overall coastal resilience is to take steps and actions to support a more sustainable and resilient local and regional economy. The case studies in section III provide a number of positive examples of economic development that reflects this new resilience. Local and regional economies will be more resilient, if they are

- *Diverse*: The coastal community or region does not rely on a single or few specific employers, companies or economic sectors.
- *Prepared*: Companies and businesses in the community are ready and have adequately planned for the natural hazards and other potentially disrupting events that could occur. A high percentage of local businesses have taken steps to reduce their vulnerability and have prepared plans that will permit them to restore functioning quickly after a major event.
- *Sustainable and green*: Businesses and economic activities should build onto the special qualities and unique resources of place. They will likely be more viable and resilient in the face of global economic changes and disruptions—for instance; if they are utilizing locally derived materials, rely on local skilled labor, and minimize their use of water, energy, and other resources in generating a product or service.
- *Supplied locally*: Companies and businesses, as well as individuals, nonprofits, and government agencies, should, where possible, utilize local and regional materials and resources. Purchasing locally produced goods and materials from locally owned stores will help keep dollars circulating and recirculating locally and help to strengthen the resilience of the local economy.
- *Community connected*: Businesses, especially service-based companies, that are more fully embedded in a community will likely be better able to respond to and rebound from a major natural event and will also serve a critical and valuable role in helping neighborhoods and communities to rebound as well.

Coastal localities can take many steps to help their economic and business sectors become more resilient, including the following:

- Partner with local businesses to help them to evaluate their exposure to natural events and to take proactive steps to reduce exposure. Project Impact, initiated under former Federal Emergency Management Agency (FEMA) director James Lee Witt, was both a program and an overarching philosophy about planning ahead for disasters. Under the FEMA program, participating local governments would initiate a collaborative community process, notably involving businesses, and agreed to undertake certain predisaster mitigation actions and steps. FEMA in turn provided participating localities with additional funds to support these predisaster mitigation efforts.
- Plan for and provide business continuity space and facilities following a major natural disaster and help (financial and technical) in allowing companies to continue to stay in a coastal community.
- Provide grants and technical assistance for preparedness and business continuity planning.
- Expedite permitting and other planning incentives that might favor those companies with a green, sustainable mission and a stronger commitment to community.
- Plan ahead of time for postdisaster business parks and areas where damaged, affected local businesses might relocate.

The coastal case studies presented in section III present a number of positive efforts to promote greater economic resilience. Palm Beach County's Post Disaster Redevelopment Plan (Palm Beach County 2004), for instance, identifies a number of specific measures intended to prevent business relocations out of that county following a major disaster event, and to generally strengthen the level of business there (see chapter 10).

The case study communities also provide good examples of places engaged in rethinking their local regional economies in ways that could make them profoundly more sustainable and resilient. Maui County, Hawaii, for instance, has adopted a community plan and vision that seeks greater self-reliance and self-sufficiency, and less dependence on materials and goods coming long distances from the mainland.

In light of approaching peak oil and other vulnerabilities, there is an emerging consensus among many in economic development circles that a vision of a local and regional economy emphasizing what is unique and special locally and seeking to utilize local resources, materials, and skills to create value and jobs has much to

Box 3.4 The Bank of Astoria, Manzanita, Oregon: Designing and Building with Local Materials and Climate in Mind

The new Manzanita branch of the Bank of Astoria (fig. 3.1), a community bank in northwest Oregon, demonstrates in compelling fashion the possibilities of designing and building in coastal areas with a focus on uniqueness of place, local climate, and utilizing mostly materials that are grown, produced, and processed locally. Designed by noted green architect Tom Bender, the resulting structure successfully reflects this coastal community's character and blends well with the surrounding landscape. As a form of organic architecture, it is at once a different look, overcoming the contemporary sameness of commercial architecture, and at the same time blending into the site and landscape. It almost seems to grow up from the site, rather than being built or erected in the usual way. The bank has many features that help to make it more sustainable: an infill location; the salvaging and reusing of native plants; 100 percent on-site stormwater retention (and the creation of an impressive water feature in the front of the building); southern orientation and a passive solar design; high energy efficiency; and a successful effort at bringing into the building extensive natural daylight, natural ventilation (a night-flushing ventilation system that utilizes the coastal Oregon climate to cool the structure), and a moss roof, among other innovative green features.

Special emphasis has been placed on sourcing local materials. The on-site trees that had to be cut down were milled and used for interior paneling and trim; shingles were sourced from a local cedar shingle mill; wood framing came from small local mills; and the structure uses so-called nonstraight woods that would otherwise not be marketable. Cabinetry and interior partition wood has also been sourced locally (Bender 2001).

Together these design features and sensibilities make for a distinctive and unusual building, and one that is pleasant to visit and work in (one expects that the productivity of bank employees is rather high, given the delightful interior spaces). These design imperatives, moreover, seem especially well suited to the kind of facility it is— a *community* bank, not a branch of a megabank, but a bank that cares about and is embedded in its community and region.

FIGURE 3.1.

The Manzanita, Oregon, branch of the Astoria Bank incorporates a number of green features and utilizes mostly building materials that have been grown, produced, and processed locally, including much of the wood and timber used in construction (e.g., roofing shingles, cabinetry). *Photo by Timothy Beatley.*

Source: Author's site visit; Bender 2001.

recommend it. Local renewable energy production, local food production, local sourcing of building and construction materials, for instance, help to prevent the outflow of local dollars, promote their recirculation, and help to buffer against dependence on outside goods, materials, energy, and so forth (and, of course, provide other benefits, such as healthier, tastier food, and a lower carbon footprint).

Box 3.4 provides an example of a new coastal building in northwest Oregon that emphasizes local climate and use of local building materials, and that provides at least a glimpse into what such a more sustainable, resilient local economic system might look in coastal areas. This community bank building utilizes locally timbered wood and wood shingles, for instance. Similarly, the case of the new sustainable coastal development at Loreto Bay, Mexico, profiled in chapter 13, emphasizes reliance on many locally derived materials, including the use of a locally made compressed-earth block. It has been estimated that in the first phase of development at least 90 percent of the mass of the buildings will have been derived from within a mile of the development.

FIGURE 3.2
Terranova's grocery store, in New Orleans, opened quickly following Hurricane Katrina and is an example of a small neighborhood-based store that listens to and effectively serves the needs of its local clientele. The store is a social gathering place and stocks foods and products desired by the neighborhood, including some food actually grown in the neighborhood. Shown here is owner Karen Terranova. *Photo by Timothy Beatley.*

Many sustainable economic activities will in turn enhance social resilience. Provision of jobs and economic opportunity locally can help to reduce some of the vulnerability seen in communities with high levels of unemployment, underemployment, and poverty (e.g., the Loreto Bay example profiled in chapter 13). At the level of an individual business or company, social stability and support can be a primary side benefit. Following Hurricane Katrina, for instance, many larger grocery stores failed to reopen, but notable smaller stores did reopen and continued to fill important social and neighborhood connection functions that larger stores cannot. One long-standing neighborhood grocer—Terranova's grocery in New Orleans (fig. 3.2)—is a case in point. Family-owned and committed to the neighborhood, the store quickly reopened and has been an informal community center and stabilizing force for neighbors following Katrina. The Terranova family has endeavored to stock goods desired by the neighborhood, and even sells food grown in the neighborhood. Perhaps most important, the store has provided a level of personal contact and continuity particularly helpful to a neighborhood coping with the many stresses of hurricane recovery.

CHAPTER 4

Barriers to
Coastal Resilience

THE BARRIERS AND OBSTACLES TO COASTAL RESILIENCE are many and significant. Some are political and economic, while others are perceptual. In any case, the development of effective local and regional land use planning strategies to enhance resilience will require an understanding of these likely obstacles, and efforts to address or otherwise overcome them.

Some of the more important obstacles identified from the literature and from coastal planning practice include the following:

- Low importance given to natural disasters and hazards vulnerability
- Limited ability or willingness to confront big issues looming in the future
- Limited resources and competing priorities
- Limited and weak coastal planning systems
- Political impediments
- Short decision-making time frames
- Concerns about protecting private property rights
- Excessive individualism
- Perceptions of upfront costs associated with resiliency measures

Each of these is described in more detail below, along with discussion of their significance as barriers to community resilience. At the end of this chapter are a few ideas and strategies for addressing and at least partially overcoming these barriers to community resilience.

Low Importance Given to Natural Disasters and Hazards Vulnerability

One major obstacle in promoting coastal hazard resilience is the low priority or low sense of urgency local officials attach to natural events like hurricanes or earthquakes. As Mileti (1999, 160) notes, managing growth to reduce hazards vulnerability is usually a lower priority than other local concerns perceived to be more important and more immediate:

> Few local governments are willing to reduce natural hazards by managing development. It is not so much that they oppose land use measures (though some do), but rather that, like individuals, they tend to view natural hazards as a *minor problem* that can take a back seat to *more pressing local concerns such as unemployment, crime, housing, and education* [emphasis mine]. Also, the costs of mitigation are immediate, while the benefits are uncertain, may not occur during the tenure of current elected officials, and are not visible (like roads or a new library).

Limited Ability or Willingness to Confront Big Issues Looming in the Future

To a certain degree it could be said that communities (coastal and otherwise) are in a kind of denial about large and looming issues such as global climate change and sea level rise, in part because the full consequences of these phenomena probably will not manifest for decades or longer, and again because of immediacy of other local matters. Despite the recent and extensive popular press and media attention given to problems of global climate change, relatively few coastal communities have given serious attention to the likely long-term consequences. As the coastal case studies in section III indicate, some coastal communities are talking about and planning for some degree of sea level rise, but few have fully grasped or taken into account likely longer-term sea level rise impacts, as well as the host of other likely effects of a dramatically changing climate.

In a 2006 survey by the International City Managers Association (ICMA) with nearly five hundred communities responding, about two-thirds (67 percent) indicated that global climate change was of low or very low priority when compared with other local issues (Walsh and Spencer 2006, 16–17). The authors of this report offer the following conclusions and speculations about why climate change isn't given greater importance in management decisions and priorities:

Climate change is not currently a high priority among local governments. Respondents' comments—that climate change is not yet a matter of concern for their elected officials; that there are other, more immediate and pressing issues; that it is not considered an important issue among the general public; and that scientific data seem uncertain or inaccurate—are strong indicators of why global warming is not a higher priority. (p. 19)

Furthermore, while the global scientific community has reached overwhelming consensus about the reality and seriousness of climate change, a combination of a skeptical (and hostile) federal administration and an overtendency on the part of press and media to provide "both points of view" has created greater scientific uncertainty among citizens and elected officials than actually exists. Popular support for addressing climate change has risen sharply in recent years, however, suggesting that the general public is beginning to shake off its apathy on this issue, and there is hope that coastal communities and their elected officials will make climate change a higher priority than it has been so far.

Limited Resources and Competing Priorities

While clearly a related obstacle, limited resources are often identified as a prime reason why a particular program or action has not been taken. The wealth and resources available to different coastal communities will certainly make a difference in determining the feasibility of certain programs.

There are often many competing demands for limited public resources. Purchasing land in a high-risk floodplain in order that it not be developed, or undertaking steps to protect and restore a coastal wetlands system, may be trumped by other local needs seen to be more pressing or of higher importance, such as education, transportation and other capital improvements, affordable housing, crime reduction, and police and fire services, among others.

Limited and Weak Coastal Planning Systems

While local planning is on a strong footing in a number of states, a weak planning system and culture exist in many coastal regions of the United States. Along the Gulf Coast, with the exception of Florida, no states mandate the preparation of local comprehensive plans, and thus local plans and planning capability are often absent (Burby 2006, 183; see also Burby 2003, 2005).

Berke and Capanella (2006, 196) also note the weak history of support for local planning by the federal government, and the federal (and state) expenditures for seawalls, beach renourishment, and other structural measures that may actually serve to exacerbate risky patterns of coastal development. As these authors state: "This approach justifies increased levels of development that might not otherwise take place without protective structures,"

What happens at the local level depends on the priority given to planning at the state level. In states where local planning is mandated, localities tend to do a better job managing growth and development. They are more likely to be resilient in their land use patterns as a result. Local commitment to planning and to implementing local plans is essential, of course, but state planning mandates do appear to make a positive difference. (e.g., see Burby and May 1997).

The nature and stringency of planning systems in place in coastal states varies greatly. According to the recent summary of state planning laws prepared through a collaboration of the Institute for Business and Home Safety and the American Planning Association, only ten coastal states mandate local planning for all or some local jurisdictions (IBHS/APA 2007, 3). Remarkably few Gulf Coast states impose any kind of planning mandate for localities (planning mandates are absent in Texas, Louisiana, Alabama, Mississippi, and Georgia). All West Coast states do impose such standards (including Oregon, profiled in chapter 9), and here the quality and effectiveness of local coastal planning is generally considered to be relatively high.

Even where a local planning mandate exists, however, few states require explicit planning for natural hazards. According to the IBHS/APA survey (2007, 3), only six coastal states require a natural hazards element, and only two (Florida and South Carolina) require the preparation of a postdisaster recovery plan or element.

But even in strong planning states such as Florida, where local comprehensive plans must include a detailed coastal element that, among other things, establishes the objectives of steering development away from coastal high-hazard areas (CHHAs) and reducing evacuation times within hurricane vulnerability zones (HVZs), evidence suggests that restraints on hazardous growth and development have not occurred. A recent study by Baker et al. (2008, 294) of nearly ninety Florida coastal jurisdictions shows substantial population increases in these hazard zones. A statewide deficit in hurricane shelter space also appears as result of this growth.

The reasons that explain the ineffectiveness of Florida localities at limiting growth in high-hazard areas are several, but all generally point up the difficulties of coastal growth management to reduce risk, even in a state with relatively strong planning mandates. According to Baker et al. (2008, 294), some Florida localities lacked an adequate definition of the hazard zones in their plans and did not have necessary policies or regulations in place to guide growth away from these zones. In other Florida localities, maximum allowable densities for these hazardous areas had been established years ago (and prior to state approval of local plans), and current growth simply reflects these earlier generous growth allocations. The limited ability of Florida's planning agency (the Department of Community Affairs) to enforce compliance is another factor, as well as the agency's giving low priority to these requirements.

Political Impediments

Limiting development in high-risk locations often results in significant political opposition, especially in coastal areas. Local elected bodies often reflect a disproportionate representation of real estate and development interests, and therefore often reflect and express a growth-oriented viewpoint.

Furthermore, good planning, and prevention of bad planning and development choices, tend not to be very visible and are rather difficult for politicians to campaign on. Tangible buildings and projects such as a new road or a community center are more visible and tend to be more easily valued and rewarded by constituents. It is not clear that there is a supportive constituency for concerted actions that *prevent* or *forestall* a disaster.

Short Decision-Making Time Frames

The typically short electoral cycle of state and local politics is often also identified as a factor in discouraging long-term resilience and reduction of vulnerability. Actions to enhance long-term resilience may not bear fruit for many years and often require concerted and steadfast investments and attention. Projects with short-term visibility and payoff will typically yield a higher political and campaign value (a new road improvement, new housing built) than steps to enhance resilience.

The short time frame of the political cycle, then, carries two limitations: resilience will require concerted long-term strategies (e.g. a steady, gradual strengthening of community institutions and capabilities, long-term land acquisition in hazardous areas, long-term ecological restoration) that few elected officials will be around to see through to completion or fruition; and, unfortunately, short-term

47

projects and decisions result in immediate political points helpful (perhaps essential) to those local leaders who aspire to longer-term service.

How to give visibility to, and political credit for, actions that enhance resilience, and how to institutionalize "resilience thinking" (as Walker and Salt 2006 aptly refer to it) are therefore critical tasks.

Concerns about Protecting Private Property

Many of the steps necessary to bring about a safer and more resilient land use pattern in a community are often at odds with the issue of private property and the ability of property owners to use their land without restrictions. While

Box 4.1 Private Property Rights and Coastal Resilience: The Case of Oregon's Measure 37

Many coastal resilience measures, especially those involving smart-growth initiatives and land use planning, will frequently bump up against concerns about private property. Landowners and developers often object to land use measures as unfair infringements on private property and as actions that serve to diminish the economic value of their land. As the U.S. Constitution (and most state constitutions as well) contains a provision that requires just compensation when private land or property is "taken" for a public purposes, landowners and developers in coastal communities frequently argue that land use regulations are so onerous and so devalue property that these actions amount to a regulatory taking (thus requiring compensation). Planners and smart-growth supporters usually argue that, to the contrary, such regulations are a legitimate exercise of the police power, even when they do result in some amount of reduction in the value of property.

Historically, much of this disagreement has been resolved in the courts, but in recent years the property rights issue has found its way prominently into state politics. Oregon represents one especially important example. Few states have had as long a serious commitment to urban growth management and land use planning as Oregon. Senate Bill 100, enacted by the state legislature in 1973, laid the groundwork for an extensive and elaborate system of statewide planning, including mandatory protection of prime forestlands and farmland, and delineation of urban growth boundaries (UGBs). Opponents of the Oregon system have always complained about the unfair burden of these land use restrictions on private property owners—for example, the farmer who is no longer able to subdivide or build on his property and whose land is thus devalued. Anger over the Oregon law by property rights groups (a group called Oregonians in Action led the charge) led to a citizens' initiative, Measure 37, requiring local governments either to compensate landowners when land use regulations devalued their property, or to waive the regulations allowing the proposed a coastal locality may attempt to "downzone" or reduce the permissible uses and density of land in a high-risk flood zone, such rezoning will usually reduce the market value of that land and result in objections from landowners. A reverence for private property and the importance given to protecting it are a significant part of U.S. history and culture and are enshrined in state and federal constitutions. Governmental restrictions on the use of private property in coastal areas (e.g., through zoning and subdivision regulations) are often objected to as unconstitutional "takings" under the Fifth Amendment of the U.S. Constitution.

In some coastal states, with Oregon as a notable example, protecting private property has emerged as a major political issue, with new limits having been

---

Box 4.1 Continued

development to proceed. This ballot measure passed in the fall of 2004, with 61 percent of Oregon voters approving the measure. The effect of the measure has been to largely nullify Oregon's famous land use controls, as most cash-strapped local governments have chosen to waive their regulations rather than pay compensation (not a single penny has been paid, in fact). By the fall of 2007, some 7,500 Measure 37 claims had been filed, covering about a half million acres of land. Billions of dollars in compensation would have been needed if local governments had chosen to actually compensate land owners.

Some observers have referred to the measure as the "Hate Your Neighbor Act" because it has fostered such anger and angst among neighboring landowners (Harden 2007). As the full effects of Measure 37 became clear, a push to overturn or correct the measure's worst disruptive effects emerged in the form of a new ballot measure-Measure 49. It passed in 2007, and substantially rolls back the regulatory limits enacted under Measure 37. More specifically, those claiming regulatory takings are now allowed to build up to three homes and no more (if allowed previously) on prime farm and forest land, and on important groundwater aquifers. Up to ten homes may be permitted (but not on farmlands, forestlands, or aquifer-restricted land) if the landowner is able to show that his or her property has suffered economic devaluation. Measure 49 also prohibits the commercial and industrial development permitted under Measure 37.

But Measure 49 certainly will not settle the property rights debate. And debate and conflict over property rights, and the appropriate limit on land use controls, have certainly not been limited to Oregon. Similar ballot measures have appeared in other states in recent years (California, Arizona, Idaho, and Washington), though most have failed to pass.

Source: Harden 2007; Mortenson 2007; Yardley 2006.

---

placed on what government can restrict or regulate without payment of compensation. This issue, and Oregon's Measure 37 specifically, are described in more detail in box 4.1.

Excessive Individualism

Americans pride themselves on a history of rugged individualism, which certainly has its virtues. However, this quality becomes problematic when it breaks down community efforts. For instance, there are many ways in which coastal resilience can only or primarily be accomplished through collective or community action. Pursuing only individual goals—whether in terms of development patterns or investments in shoreline protection or recovery and reconstruction following a disaster—can result in less-than-optimal social outcomes. Social sharing of resources and expertise, an ethic of helping others, and a rich and robust set of social networks and resources are often what is required to create the conditions of resilience, yet excessive individualism and a go-it-alone view of the world may represent a large obstacle indeed.

Perception of High Upfront Costs for Resilience Measures

While coastal resilience and mitigation measures usually entail additional upfront costs, the economic return is often substantial. The evidence is pretty compelling that the return on investment in resilience projects and initiatives is substantial. The Multihazard Mitigation Council (MMC) of the National Institute of Building Sciences completed in 2005 one of the most comprehensive studies of the economic benefits of hazard mitigation (MMC 2005). More specifically, the study documents both the future savings from individual mitigation projects funded by Federal Emergency Management Agency (FEMA) hazard mitigation grants and the community benefits associated with mitigation activities and programs. The results show that investments in mitigation are returned fourfold in the form of savings. Thus, for every dollar spent on a mitigation project, a savings of four dollars will be experienced. The study concludes that the savings to the U.S. Treasury of federally funded mitigation are also substantial.

The MMC's study of community benefits is especially interesting, and shows that there are often many other more indirect and less quantifiable benefits at the community level that accrue from funding mitigation projects (MMC 2005, 5):

The Community analysis found the FEMA mitigation grants are cost-effective, often leading to additional non-federally funded mitigation activities, and have the greatest benefits in communities that have institutionalized hazard mitigation programs. In the communities studied, FEMA mitigation grants were a significant part of the community's mitigation history. The study found the FEMA-funded mitigation activities brought about the most additional non-federally-funded mitigation benefits if the FEMA grant was of the sort that helped to institutionalize mitigation in the community. Interviewees reported that the grants were important in reducing community risks, preventing future damages, and increasing a community's capability to reduce losses from natural hazards. Most interviewees believed that the grants permitted their communities to attain mitigation goals that might not otherwise have been reached and that the mitigation benefits of the activities funded by the grants went beyond what could actually be measured quantitatively (e.g., increased community awareness, esprit de corps, and peace of mind).

Ideas for Overcoming Barriers to Coastal Resilience

While these obstacles together suggest the difficulties planners and others face in making coastal communities more resilient, all hope is not lost. Rather, there are a number of potential tactics and strategies that might be used to successfully, or at least partially, overcome them. While by no means an exhaustive list, here are a few beginning ideas:

- Look for opportunities to integrate hazard reduction and coastal resilience into other community projects that may have stronger public support (e.g., designing a school so that it supports resilience in its location, functioning, and curriculum).
- Insert references to future vulnerability into current policy and planning discussions (what will be the cumulative impact of this pattern of land use, say, in a hundred years?).
- Employ land use tools and community planning techniques that help to minimize objection and opposition by private property owners and developers (e.g., techniques like transfer of development rights that help to offset the impacts of land use regulations, or incentives such as density bonuses for more resilient buildings and developments). (See chapter 7 for more detail.)
- Find creative ways to make resilience visible and tangible (e.g., exercises that show how much impact a storm would have had if development in a floodplain had been allowed).

• Build and support local constituents for resilience (many local groups, from land conservation organizations to taxpayer groups concerned about government spending, might find a common voice around resilience).
• Incorporate natural disasters and disaster preparedness into elementary and high school curricula as an antidote to local apathy (see section III for some examples—e.g., education about tsunami hazards along the northwest Oregon coast).

Because of the significant political, social, and economic obstacles to achieving coastal resilience, a longer view is required for tackling tough issues such as sea level rise, as well as infrequent yet devastating events such as tsunamis, often issues for which there are few coastal constituencies clamoring for action. Overcoming the usual narrow, short-term perspectives with the emphasis given to low-cost, easy answers (and often inadequate solutions) is a challenge indeed. The emergence of truly resilient coastal communities will require education, leadership, and efforts at building constituencies and popular support for resiliency measures.

CHAPTER 5

Understanding the Political Setting and Context

URBAN GROWTH—ITS LOCATION, QUALITY, pace, and form—is in any community a function of an often complex interaction between actors and groups pursuing their ends, economic and political processes, and expressed values and ideology.

Understanding Coastal Growth Politics

Many different political models have been put forth to help conceptualize and explain how local politics work, and there are many competing theories about who ultimately has the power and whose interests ultimately prevail at the local level.

One useful model is the *systems* view of local politics, which understands a political outcome (local, state, or national) as the result of a complex interaction between the interests and behaviors of specific actors and stakeholders; the political distribution of power in a community; the political process itself; and the many political, economic, and normative factors of the local "environment" that help to shape and frame discussion. Political scientist David Easton (1965) is known for developing this model, which helps to explain much of what happens. In Easton's model, local coastal ordinances and programs are the result of one or more individuals or groups' initiating a proposal or action, and the outcome is the result of the comparative balance of positive and negative pressures exerted by groups in the community on the political process. The political process converts these proposals into actions (adoption or denial), and program funds and urban resources are allocated to their implementation. The outcome—a program that might influence coastal resilience (say, adoption of a new floodplain management standard)—in turn influences future decisions through a feedback loop (perhaps the ordinance's economic impact is viewed by local developers as too onerous, and they work to weaken the program). On the other hand, the feedback loop might provide new positive support—say, for example, the floodplain ordinance is shown to work well, and in the end is perceived not as an overly onerous imposition on developers, but as a sensible safeguard actually supported and rewarded in the marketplace. A key point is that coastal planning and policy making are not static, with definitive beginning and end points, but are rather ongoing and dynamic processes, with each project or decision or program influencing future policy making. The larger "environment" in Easton's model represents the social, cultural, and environmental backdrops—the larger conditions that tend to shape and constrain proposals made and the positive and negative supports that line up around a proposal.

Classically, the explanation for why a smart-growth law or program passes or fails hinges on the relative power and resources of different factions and interest groups in the community (e.g., real estate interests, environmental groups, neighborhood associations) with often quite different points of view. Development interests often have substantially more resources to exert (money, advertising), and the legitimacy of their position is often enhanced by the background values and political culture of the community.

Specific events can also influence the political viability of smart-growth or resilience measures. Historically, following major disaster events, we have seen significant windows of opportunity open up to adopt more stringent building codes and hazard mitigation standards. The unified building code used in California has some of the strongest seismic building standards anywhere and has been gradually and repeatedly strengthened in response to earthquake disasters in that state. Major hurricanes can have a similar focusing function and can enhance the political viability of stronger resilience measures and programs, at least for a time (the windows of opportunity do eventually close). Postdisaster rebuilding plans, prepared in advance of a hurricane or other coastal disaster, are often argued from the standpoint of taking advantage of such a window of opportunity.

Actors and Stakeholders

In the systems model of local politics, the relative power of individuals and groups in the community is important, and most acknowledge that the power is shifting and dynamic. Under a pluralist view of local power, stakeholders share power, and, given the intensity of an issue or proposal, one group or interest may be more powerful than another and its views prevail.

It is often argued that a failing of the American political system is that it is largely issue and crisis driven, and is often overly self-interested. For instance, a community group may mobilize in response to a proposal to build an affordable housing project that they perceive to jeopardize their neighborhood quality and property values. It is harder, though not impossible, to activate and engage citizens and stakeholders in actions that relate to the larger public good, the larger quality and sustainability and resilience of the community and region. The local coastal planning process, ideally, is a collaborative process involving all relevant parties (see box 5.1).

Box 5.1 Key Actors in the Local Coastal Development Process

Developers and builders
Land use planners and planning bodies
Banks and lending institutions
Local elected officials
Neighborhood and community groups
Environmental and other local interest groups
State and federal government resource agencies
Public utilities and infrastructure providers
Schools and school districts
Business associations/chambers of commerce
Media

External Forces

Economic and Social Trends

A number of external forces impact the planning and growth management outcomes at the local level in coastal areas. Some of these issues and forces originate outside the local community, for example:

- Larger macroeconomic trends (e.g., interest rates, changes in the value of the U.S. dollar that might affect international coastal tourism, investment trends, increases in the price of gasoline)
- Larger social trends and patterns (e.g., changes in the workweek and in the availability of recreational time)

- Social perceptions and perceptual changes (e.g., is it safe to live and recreate on the coast? is it cool or fashionable?)
- Fiscal and economic policies at state and federal levels (e.g., federal mortgage interest deduction availability for second-home purchases, federal flood insurance, federal disaster assistance)

Table 5.1 Comparison of Planning Requirements in Selected Coastal States

	LOCAL PLANS MANDATED?	HAZARDS ELEMENT MANDATORY?	DISCRETE HAZARDS ELEMENT?	DOES STATE SPECIFY OR SUGGEST ELEMENTS OF LOCAL PLANS?	POSTDISASTER RECOVERY PLAN?	STRENGTH OF STATE (FROM 1—3: ROLE 1 = WEAK, 2 = SIGNIFICANT, 3 = SUBSTANTIAL)
California	Yes	Yes	Yes[1]	Specify	No	3
Florida	Yes	Yes	Yes	Both	Yes	3
Hawaii	Yes[2]	No	No	Suggest	No	3
North Carolina	Yes[3]	Yes[4]	Yes[5]	Specify[6]	No	3 for coastal, weak role otherwise (split judgment)
Oregon	Yes	Yes	Yes	Specify	No	3
South Carolina	Yes[7]	Yes	Yes	Specify	Yes	2
Texas	No	No	No	No	No	1
Virginia	Yes	No	No[8]	Specify[9]	No	1
Alabama	No	No	No	Specify[10]	No	1

Source: Institute for Business and Home Safety and American Planning Association 2007.

TABLE NOTES FROM IBHS/APA 2007:

1. Delaware has a separate code section on planning for each of its three counties.

2. Hawaii's state plan includes a series of mandatory comprehensive plans for all four counties

3. This is a split judgment. Under the Coastal Areas Management Act, North Carolina plays a substantial role in planning for coastal counties, but a weaker role elsewhere.

4. The requirements apply only to coastal counties.

5. The requirements apply only to coastal counties.

6. The specifications apply only to coastal counties under the Coastal Areas Management Act. There are no specifications elsewhere.

7. In coastal areas, local governments must prepare beachfront management plans. If they fail to do so, the state must impose its own plan.

8. The statute simply mentions flood plain and drainage as one type of area designation and as part of a land-use study

9. The requirements or suggestions are merely a list of items in a single paragraph without any further delineations of what those items should contain, nor any details on how those considerations should be organized into discrete elements.

10. The requirements or suggestions are merely a list of items in a single paragraph without any further delineations of what those items should contain, nor any details on how those considerations should be organized into discrete elements.

These larger forces will tend to shape the context of resilience decision making at the local level, and may make a resilience program more or less feasible depending on their direction. Higher insurance rates (or the loss of insurance availability in coastal areas) will tend to make adoption of resilience measures easier, while generous disaster assistance and other coastal development incentives will work in the opposite direction. Rising oil prices will make more compact smart-growth patterns more attractive, as will changing perceptions of what constitutes a desirable living environment (perhaps a rise in interest in smaller homes and apartments in more walkable neighborhoods).

State Planning and Hazard Mitigation Mandates

Often what explains the planning and regulatory provisions at the local level are mandates or requirements at the state level. In most states where good local planning occurs, there is a state mandate for preparing these plans and often very detailed requirements for what must be in these plans, as well as state review of their content and quality.

Table 5.1 compares and contrasts planning requirements in several coastal states, showing the wide variation in context faced by coastal localities. For example, coastal localities in Florida and Oregon are expected to do much more in the way of planning and development management than coastal localities in Virginia or Alabama. The lack of state mandates or assistance in some places, and the lack of state "cover" that progressive local officials and advocates of smart growth and growth management often say is so valuable, make the planning accomplishments in these places all the more impressive.

Local governments in states that mandate local planning tend to manage growth and development change more effectively and thus are more likely to encourage resilient land use patterns. State planning mandates do appear to make a positive difference, though local commitment to planning and to implementing local plans is essential as well (e.g., see Burby and May 1997).

Political Culture and Ideology

It is obvious to even the casual observer that there are dramatic differences in the planning and environmental management standards and emphasis in the different U.S. states and regions. We are a diverse country with many regional differences in history, culture, religion, and settlement patterns, and these have given rise to differing background ideologies. Daniel Elazar (1984) was one of the first

57

to analyze and write about these ideological differences, describing them in terns of variations in "political culture." In areas of the country such as the Northeast, and especially New England, there is a long tradition of collective action and a sense that individual choices and behavior must be constrained by what is in the best interest of the larger community good. In contrast, in the Intermountain West and the South, and in states like Texas, there is a much greater emphasis on individual rights and the unencumbered ability to use one's property as one sees fit. Differences in political culture explain much of why planning and growth management is easier or harder in some places than in others. However, underlying political culture is not definitive in explaining an outcome; rather, it is a contextual factor in understanding local coastal growth management dynamics.

Development decisions in the coastal zone occur through a complex interplay of local political actions and decisions and larger social, economic, and political forces that serve to shape and contextualize these local decisions. Any specific resilience policy or action, or any specific development project, will involve numerous stakeholders—landowners and developers, citizen activists and community organizations, planners and elected officials, among others—whose motivations and values about coastal development will often be sharply different. Any move toward resilience will demand a new appreciation for and understanding of these political dynamics, and efforts to craft planning programs and measures that acknowledge these political realities.

CHAPTER 6

Principles of Coastal Resilience

WHAT FOLLOWS IS A SET OF BROAD PRINCIPLES to help citizens and decision makers alike in coastal communities begin to think about how to design and plan for greater resilience. These principles are not mutually exclusive but are reinforcing and complementary. They are synthesized and drawn from several key sources, including the coastal planning and resilience literature, insights gleaned from interviews of key coastal planners and leaders, and the author's extensive professional experience working in coastal planning.

Take a Long-Term, Multiscaled Approach

It perhaps goes without saying that coastal resilience requires a long-term temporal frame of reference. Attention should be given to short-term problems and solutions (buying that backup generator), but longer-term trends and problems must be confronted. How will sea level rise or drought and climate conditions change the nature of the coast and impact coastal communities in fifty years, a hundred years, or even longer?

Coastal resilience requires action at several different geographical scales: from the individual or household level all the way to regional and bioregional scale. Coastal resilience is best thought of as a *nested* planning and policy system: actions can and must be taken at the individual level (e.g., strong home construction standards), but many things must occur at broader geographical scales (regional land use and growth patterns that steer population and development away from high-risk locations, regional resilience systems of green infrastructure).

Create a Compelling Vision of the Future

Any coastal resilience strategy is doomed to ultimate failure unless citizens and businesses and public officials embrace it as a positive and compelling vision of the future. Developing an effective strategy is partly about undertaking community dialogue and frank discussion about the community's future exposure and vulnerability, and partly about putting the pieces together in a manner that conveys this positive future in a visual and compelling way. Is this a community you and your family want to live in, a place that values the unique and special place attributes? It is necessary to have a vision that conveys the possibility of dramatically improving quality of life and which at the same time reduces the vulnerability to natural disaster.

Guide Growth and Development Away from High-Risk Locations

Avoidance is ultimately the most effective and sensible approach to resilience in the face of physical forces. Land use planning and a variety of implementation tools from zoning to transfer of development rights to conservation easements and land acquisition can be used to steer development and people *away from* and *out of harm's way*. A variety of coastal hazards are already mapped and delimited—high-erosion zones, floodplains, earthquake fault zones, and high-slope areas subject to slides and mass movements—and ideally these areas should be left undeveloped, or developed at low densities. These are areas, moreover, where opportunities will exist for more resilient sustainable relocation following a hurricane, earthquake, or other disaster event.

Ensure That Critical Facilities Are Located Out of or Away from High-Risk Locations

The ability to weather a major natural event will depend greatly on the design and siting of critical facilities—these include basic infrastructure such as municipal sewage collection and treatment; water supply systems; roads and highways; shelters; and hospitals and critical medical facilities. The first priority ought to be to ensure that these facilities are sited to avoid or minimize exposure. For example, as discussed in the Palm Beach County case study in chapter 10, Florida's hazards planning system prohibits the siting of new critical facilities in coastal high-hazard zones. Other case studies (e.g., Cannon Beach, Oregon, in chapter 9) illustrate the importance of locating critical facilities and response functions such as fire stations outside of high-risk locations (fig. 6.1). Roads and highways can be elevated, schools and shelters can be strengthened, and facilities and infrastructure can generally be designed and built in ways that reduce future exposure.

Plan Ahead for a Resilient Recovery and Growth

Resilience requires advance planning and being prepared ahead of an event. This means thinking systemically before the storm or earthquake about how the community might rebuild and redevelop in ways that will reduce exposure and enhance long-term resilience, and that will allow for adaptation and learning and taking advantage of unusual postdisaster opportunities. Are there especially dangerous areas where rebuilding should not occur? How will the community ensure that local businesses are able to recover and cope, and where will they function and operate during the period of reconstruction and rebuilding?

FIGURE 6.1
The Cannon Beach Fire Station was relocated from its high tsunami-vulnerable location downtown to a safer higher-elevation site. Community resilience can be enhanced by locating or relocating critical facilities and response functions out of and away from high-hazard locations.
Photo by Timothy Beatley.

New planning instruments and approaches will be helpful in taking this longer-term view, including the preparation of disaster recovery and rebuilding plans, and long-term growth and land use modeling that will help to show what the implications are of maintaining a business-as-usual approach to community and regional growth.

Preserve and Restore Ecosystems and Ecological Infrastructure

A city or region's natural ecosystems and green infrastructure represent one of the clearest and most effective lines of defense against many natural disasters. Protecting natural coastal marshes and wetlands that soak up and absorb floodwaters, dune and beach systems that act as natural seawalls, and trees and healthy tree canopies that shield homes against wind are all positive steps that will have long-term resilience.

Promote a Diverse Local Economy

The ability of a city or community to spring back quickly to a natural disaster will depend heavily on the business sector and the extent to which businesses are able to reopen expeditiously. A local economic base characterized by a diverse number of locally owned stores and businesses committed to the community and region will promote local sustainability overall and will also likely make the community more resilient following a hurricane or other significant natural event. Campanella (2006, 143) makes this point: "A city with a robust, diversified economy, for example, will rebound much more quickly than a city with a narrowly specialized or weak economy." The U.S. Green Building Council's "New Orleans Principles" strongly advocate support of locally owned sustainable businesses, including reconstruction-centered businesses, waste-based industries, solar roofing and other sustainable businesses, agriculture, and ecotourism (USBC 2005).

A community will also respond more quickly and resiliently if it is prepared in advance to assist local businesses in staying, recovering, and dealing with the host of issues that they will confront. Of course, the extent that businesses have planned for disaster ahead of time will ensure that residents are in turn able to recover more quickly.

Work Toward a Landscape of Resilience

In line with the principle of multiscale strategies, urban and suburban land-scapes can be designed in many ways to be more resilient in the long run. Use of low-impact development (LID) and other innovative urban greening and stormwater management strategies are perhaps the best examples. Low-impact development can be achieved with green rooftops (fig. 6.2), reduced and permeable paving, rain gardens, xeriscaping (planting yards, gardens, and public spaces with drought-resistant native plants), and other natural and green features. In many parts of the United States where drought and summer heat are significant natural events, these techniques can help to make urban land-scapes more resilient.

The American Society of Landscape Architects (ASLA), in collaboration with the Lady Bird Johnson Wildflower Center and the U.S. Botanic Garden, has been developing a comprehensive set of guidelines and standards for sustainable land-

FIGURE 6.2

Increasingly, coastal communities are utilizing creative new stormwater management strategies, broadly described as low-impact development (LID). These techniques include use of trees, bioswales and rain gardens, and green rooftops. The new Ballard branch of the Seattle Public Library incorporates an extensive green rooftop planted with fourteen different species of grasses native to the region. *Photo by Timothy Beatley.*

scapes that will likely prove highly useful in designing coastal landscapes. Known as the Sustainable Sites Initiative, the project emphasizes preserving soil, avoiding chemicals, using native plant species, designing landscapes to minimize consumption of energy and water, and utilizing sustainable planting materials (local materials with low embodied energy) (Venhaus 2008). A landscape rating system similar to the U.S. Green Building Council's Leadership in Energy and Environmental Design (LEED) rating system for buildings is envisioned and will likely be integrated into LEED. A preliminary report identifying some two hundred sustainable landscape design strategies has been released, with a final set of guidelines to be issued in 2009 (ASLA 2008).

Design and Build Decentralized Resilient Infrastructures

Consistent with the notion of "passive survivability" for individual homes and buildings (see below), emphasis can and should be given to replacing highly vulnerable centralized and "rigid" infrastructure systems—centralized power production and distribution—with distributed and decentralized systems that reduce exposure and vulnerability during a natural disaster and that also provide robustness and redundancy.

Greater reliance on localized energy production from photovoltaics and other building and neighborhood-based renewables, for instance, will help reduce vulnerability following a storm or earthquake, and reduce the likely time of service interruption. On-site stormwater collection and treatment through low-impact development techniques (rain gardens, green rooftops) again reduce reliance on centralized stormwater collection systems vulnerable to damage and failure. Many other examples of more sustainable and decentralized forms of coastal infrastructure can be cited.

Plan for Long-Term Community Sustainability

A desire for a more sustainable future is one increasingly expressed at individual and collective levels, and community sustainability has been gaining much traction in recent years. Sustainability and resilience are usually mutually reinforcing and should be viewed as such. Protecting landscapes and natural systems, a goal of sustainability for many different reasons, usually in turn helps to preserve the long-term resilience of these systems and the human and built environments around them. Designing energy-efficient homes and buildings will often tend to make them more resilient in the face of natural events, as well as help to make the broader coastal region more resilient through reducing energy loads, reducing the chances of brownouts, and allowing for a transition to cleaner, healthier, and more renewable forms of energy production (fig. 6.3). Investing in greater community food security (e.g., programs for supporting local farms and farmers, community markets, etc.) will advance a number of sustainability goals and also enhance the resilience of the community in the face of a future major event or perturbation (e.g., a hurricane or a rapid decline in global oil supplies).

FIGURE 6.3
The Villages at Loreto Bay, in Loreto Bay, Mexico, is a new coastal resort that incorporates a number of sustainable features, including renewable energy, use of local materials, and extensive ecological restoration. The homes are designed to facilitate natural ventilation and cooling through interior courtyards and fountains, and kitchen cupolas that draw cool air through the structures. *Photo courtesy of Villages at Loreto Bay.*

Think Holistically

The ability of a community to respond to and adapt successfully to a major natural disaster requires a level of holistic thinking not yet common, yet disasters touch every aspect of daily life and every environmental, social, and economic aspect of a community and region. Resilience is about a number of nontraditional planning subjects—for instance, the availability of food and community food systems, and the provision of energy and water.

There is another sense in which resilience requires holistic thinking, and that has to do with the need to address underlying community trends that exacerbate social and economic vulnerability in the face of disasters. These include existing inadequacies in housing quality and availability, underlying poverty, and food insecurity. Enhancing and building long-term resilience in the face of natural events will also require a concerted effort to address the background and underlying patterns of vulnerability that are predictive of postevent conditions.

Design for Passive Survivability and Sustainability

Homes and buildings should be designed to ensure "passive survivability"—that is, they should be able to survive the loss of essential services in the event of a natural disaster. At the level of an individual home or building, the idea is in many ways to return to the old design ideas (e.g., utilizing rising hot air to pull air through a home or structure). Homes used to be constructed with high ceilings, utilizing natural ventilation and stack effect, with natural light that permitted their functioning as living spaces in the absence of electricity.

Passive survivability is a major theme in "The New Orleans Principles," a set of principles and proposals derived from a three-day charrette convened by the U.S. Green Building Council in 2005 (see box 6.1). As recommended in the document (USBC 2005), such buildings

> should be designed to maintain survivable thermal conditions without air conditioning or supplemental heat through the use of cooling-load avoidance strategies, natural ventilation, highly efficient building envelopes, and passive solar design. Schools and other public buildings should be designed and built with natural daylighting so that they can be used without power during the daytime. Co-locate healthcare facilities with schools as part of the community anchor and to strengthen survivability.

Box 6.1 The New Orleans Principles

1. *Respect the rights of all citizens of New Orleans.* Displaced citizens who wish to return to New Orleans should be afforded the opportunity to return to healthy, livable, safe, and secure neighborhoods of choice.

2. *Restore natural protections of the greater New Orleans region.* Sustain and restore the coastal and floodplain ecosystems and urban forests that support and protect the environment, economy, communities, and culture of southern Louisiana, and that contribute greatly to the economy and well-being of the nation.

3. *Implement an inclusive planning process.* Build a community-centered planning process that uses local talent and makes sure that the voices of all New Orleanians are heard. This process should be an agent of change and renewal for New Orleans.

4. *Value diversity in New Orleans.* Build on the traditional strength of New Orleans neighborhoods, encourage mixed uses and diverse housing options, and foster communities of varied incomes, mixed age groups, and a racial diversity. Celebrate the unique culture of New Orleans, including its food, music, and art.

5. *Protect the city of New Orleans.* Expand or build a flood protection infrastructure that serves multiple uses. Value, restore, and expand the urban forests, wetlands, and natural systems of the New Orleans region that protect the city from wind and storms.

6. *Embrace smart development.* Maintain and strengthen the New Orleans tradition of compact, connected, mixed-use communities. Provide residents and visitors with multiple transportation options. Look to schools for jumpstarting neighborhood redevelopment and for rebuilding strong communities in the city.

7. *Honor the past; build for the future.* In the rebuilding of New Orleans, honor the history of the city while creating 21st century buildings that are durable, affordable, inexpensive to operate, and healthy to live in. Through codes and other measures, ensure that all new buildings are built to high standards of energy, structural, environmental, and human health performance.

8. *Provide for passive survivability.* Homes, schools, public buildings, and neighborhoods should be designed and built or rebuilt to serve as livable refuges in the event of crisis or breakdown of energy, water, and sewer systems.

9. *Foster locally owned, sustainable businesses.* Support existing and new local businesses built on a platform of sustainability that will contribute to a stronger and more diverse local economy.

10. *Focus on the long term.* All measures related to rebuilding and ecological restoration, even short-term efforts, must be undertaken with explicit attention to the long-term solutions.

Source: U.S. Green Building Council, undated, "LEED Rating Systems," found at http://www.usgbc.org/Display Page.aspx?CMSPageID=222 (accessed March 31, 2009).

Other specific recommendations include installation of emergency water systems and rooftop rainwater harvesting systems in homes and public buildings, backup electricity generation for municipal sewage systems, and installation of solar electric and solar water heating systems. (See also the passive survivability checklist in appendix I.)

In addition to designing passive survivability at the building level, *neighborhood* passive survivability should also be considered. Extending this idea might suggest some additional elements to take into account: fruit trees and edible landscaping, though subject to damage in flood events, might serve as a part of a resilient neighborhood food system when, as in New Orleans, it may take months for conventional grocery stores to reopen or restock their wares sufficiently. There are undoubtedly other food dimensions to passive survivability, and so this concept should be understood as broadly as possible.

Promote Social Resilience by Nurturing Critical Social Networks and Institutions

A coastal community has little hope of achieving or substantially advancing resilience without adequate attention to the social realm. Indeed, a resilient coastal community is one that has a strong social system and a strong network of social relationships. We know that in times of stress and crises, these social networks and relationships can provide crucial buffering opportunities. Research increasingly shows the value of deep and extensive friendship patterns in recovering from disease (e.g., lower mortality and higher recovery rates for cancer patients with deeper, more extensive friendship patterns). Friendships, knowing one's neighbors, and having well-developed patterns of community and neighborhood socializing and sharing represent significant and important ways that a community can be prepared for a future natural disaster or crisis.

Resilience in recovery and reconstruction will depend heavily on this social realm. As Campanella (2006, 142) notes:

> Broken highways can be mended, buildings repaired and made taller than before, communications systems patched back together. But cities are more than the sum of their buildings. They are also concatenations of social and cultural matter, and it is often this that endows a place with its defining essence and identity. It is one thing for a city's buildings to be reduced to rubble; it is much worse for a city's communal institutions and social fabric to be torn apart as well. To enable total recovery, familial, social and religious networks of survivors and evacuees must be reconnected.

Putnam and others refer to this as the "social capital" of a community, and building up and strengthening this capital may be as important a strategy for enhancing resilience as strengthening and building up the homes and buildings (see Putnam 2000; Putnam, Feldstein, and Cohen 2004). Social capital "includes all the formal and informal networks among people: family, friends, and neighbors, as well as social institutions at all levels, like churches, social clubs, local, state, and national governments, NGOs, and international organizations" (Costanza, Mitsch, and Day 2006, 318; see also Briggs 2004).

Many programs, strategies, and tools are available to coastal communities attempting to strengthen these mechanisms of social resilience. Even the land use and urban form of a community can help to strengthen social resilience. New Urbanism as an approach for designing and building in coastal regions has aroused much interest in recent years. Neighborhoods that utilize design principles of the traditional American town or small city are increasingly common: homes are closer together on smaller lots, with an emphasis on sidewalks and walkability and on traditional design features, such as porches, that help to facilitate social interaction as well as physical activity. Some of the more innovative and impressive examples of New Urbanism can be found in coastal communities (e.g., the Villages at Loreto Bay, Mexico, and Noisette, in North Charleston, South Carolina, both of which are profiled in section III). While undoubtedly a step in the right direction, many New Urbanist communities suffer from bad location (often on greenfield sites, in very car-dependent locations) and have difficulty overcoming the larger forces that prevent a richer social life and realm (e.g., workaholic patterns, individualism, emphasis on auto-mobility). Nevertheless, more compact patterns of community growth and development where walking is possible and encouraged, and where public spaces are abundant and a public sphere is nurtured, have the potential to enhance coastal resilience in significant ways.

A robust and extensive set of social networks and institutions will help in effective recovery and will also allow a community to resiliently weather the event and to perhaps inoculate against its most severe impacts. Extensive and healthy "social capital" will in theory assist in each disaster phase. For instance, if communication and social networks are strong among neighbors, locally owned neighborhood stores, and religious institutions, evacuation may be more effective in the event of a hurricane. Following a major event, most immediate survival and response concerns may be alleviated through such networks and institutions, as well as long-term recovery.

Community helping networks can do much to ensure recovery following a natural event. In New Orleans, food availability has been and continues to be a major issue. Many residents still lack access not only to food ingredients but also to functioning kitchens in which to cook the food. In some parts of the city, a culture of neighborhood cooking has stepped in to fill this post-Katrina need.

Encourage an Active, Healthy Community and Citizenry

Coastal populations and communities that suffer from high rates of obesity, sedentary lifestyles, and unhealthy diets will not be very resilient in the face of future stressful and challenging natural events such as hurricanes and earthquakes and likely will not cope or respond well. One of the best and most effective strategies for promoting long-term community resilience is to encourage and facilitate healthier lifestyles, including abundant opportunities for outside recreational activities, such as community and neighborhood land use patterns that allow for walking

FIGURE 6.4
Coastal communities can enhance health and resilience by providing sufficient opportunities for residents to walk, bicycle, and in other ways maintain physically active lifestyles. The seawall promenade that encircles the city of Vancouver, British Columbia, is a major recreational resource and amenity for residents there. *Photo by Timothy Beatley.*

and bicycling (fig. 6.4). Resilience, then, will be enhanced through investments in such things as bike and walking trails, water and beach access points, sidewalks, and pedestrian and biking facilities of various kinds.

Engage the Community by Nurturing Forward-Looking Leadership

Coastal resilience will depend on the active involvement and participation of the community; plans for community resilience (including the community's land use plan and plan to guide future development in more resilient ways) will require community "buy-in" to be effective and for any hope of long-term implementation. Mechanisms for citizen participation and community engagement, moreover, are necessary for deepening a sense of rootedness and caring for place, a sense of bonding and trust between and among residents.

Coastal resilience can also be advanced through forward-looking and responsible leadership, especially from elected officials. Many bold mitigation and resilience measures succeeded because they were championed by a mayor or county commissioner. Such strong leaders have the potential to form coalitions, build bridges, and work to overcome the usual objections and political impediments that exist to thinking and acting in ways that take the long view and that advance a larger and broader notion of the public interest.

This chapter has identified some key principles of coastal resiliency. These principles should not be viewed as exhaustive or definitive but rather as a first attempt at articulating some principles to guide development and planning in coastal environments. Each principle is relatively general, and its precise application or meaning "on the ground" will vary. The main intent is to stimulate thinking and discussion about what resilience requires of us: think of the principles listed here as starting points from which to modify, adapt, and develop your own specific community resiliency principles.

CHAPTER 7

Tools and Techniques for Enhancing and Strengthening Coastal Resilience

WHILE EACH COASTAL COMMUNITY and region has its own special opportunities to enhance resilience, the options and tools available are many. Many different steps can be taken, but the design and planning of a community's land use pattern, infrastructural investments, and built environments can be some of the most effective in advancing resilience. Much of what follows focuses on such design and planning, as well as the ways in which local and regional ecosystems can be protected and restored.

Key Elements of Resilient Coastal Land Use

Working to bring about more resilient and sustainable land use patterns ought to be one of the highest priorities of coastal communities, and there is now a growing consensus about what these resilient land use patterns should look like. Some key elements of resilient coastal land use include the following:

- Population and development should be located, to the extent possible, *outside of and away from high-risk coastal hazard zones*. Buildings should be set back a substantial distance from coastal shorelines, and no or very little development should be allowed within 100-year flood zones.
- Coastal growth patterns should *build onto the historic patterns of towns and villages* that typically exist in coastal regions. Relatively compact, mixed-use villages and towns dot the American coastal landscape from New England

73

to the South, and can serve as the linchpins of a more sustainable and resilient growth pattern. Infill development and redevelopment of brownfield, greyfield, and previously committed land should be favored over greenfield locations.

- Coastal land use patterns should be *compact and walkable* and simultaneously conserve land, reduce car dependence and energy consumption, and allow the possibility of healthier lifestyles and living patterns.
- Coastal land use policies and regulations should be enacted to *protect, preserve, and restore ecological systems* and natural features such as wetlands, forests, and riparian systems. These provide valuable natural services and also help mitigate natural disasters such as coastal storms and flooding.
- Land use patterns and community design should incorporate *direct access to nature and natural systems.* The emotional and psychological benefits provided by parks, trails, and water access points are an integral part of creating a healthy coastal community.
- Community land use patterns should *promote social and community interaction* by creating pedestrian-friendly streets, sidewalks, and gathering places and a vibrant public realm that includes "third places" such as parks and plazas, farmers' markets, and the like. Land use patterns should also help to strengthen place bonds by recognizing and nurturing features that make the community distinctive, such as preserving historic buildings and connections to a community's past.
- Critical facilities such as hospitals and police and fire stations should be *sited outside of high-risk locations,* and in places where in the event of a major community disruption they will remain functional. Water and sewage treatment plants should be sited outside of high-risk zones and designed similarly to operate after a disaster event.
- Essential community lifelines and infrastructure should be designed and integrated into a community's land use to *reduce exposure* and vulnerability and to *ensure operability* during and after community disruptions. Examples include elevating roads, placing power lines underground, and shifting to distributed energy systems that minimize large power outages.
- Land use patterns should emphasize the benefits of *green infrastructure* over conventional infrastructure that will be more likely to fail in disaster events. Green infrastructure might include stormwater management; small-scale on-site stormwater collection and retention; green rooftops and living walls and building facades; and trees and tree canopy coverage, which offer cooling and shading benefits that minimize reliance on mechanical and energy-intensive approaches.

The design and planning of a coastal community's land use patterns can influence its long-term resilience in both *direct* and *indirect* ways. By keeping new development out of high-risk flood zones, for instance, and by preserving and restoring natural mitigation features such as coastal wetlands, a community can directly reduce future exposure and vulnerability to destructive events such as hurricanes. However, land use planning also influences resilience in many more indirect ways. If by designing communities that are compact and walkable and that exhibit a high degree of connectedness, stronger social ties and networks are created and residents are more physically active and healthier, these outcomes will help to "immunize" a community in the face of future disruptive events, and therefore the resilience and adaptive capacity of the community will be greater.

Box 7.1 Land Use Tools for Coastal Resilience

COMMUNITY PLANS AND PLAN MAKING
- Local comprehensive plan (or general plan or land use plan)
- Hazard mitigation plan (now mandated under the federal Disaster Mitigation Act of 2000)
- Postdisaster recovery plan
- Sustainability action plan

ZONING AND DEVELOPMENT REGULATIONS
- Traditional zoning and subdivision ordinances
- Urban growth boundaries (UGB), designated growth areas
- Clustering standards
- Conservation and hazard overlays
- Coastal and shoreline setbacks
- Planned unit development (PUD) provisions
- Traditional neighborhood design (TND) ordinances
- Form-based codes

LAND AND PROPERTY ACQUISITION
- Fee-simple acquisition
- Less-than-fee-simple acquisition: conservation easement, purchase of development rights

- Land banks; land trusts
- Community land trusts (CLTs)
- Community forests
- Relocation and acquisition of hazardous areas pre- and postdisaster

PUBLIC FACILITIES AND CAPITAL IMPROVEMENTS POLICIES
- Capital improvements program (CIP)
- Urban service boundaries
- Adequate facilities standards
- Impact fees

TAXATION AND FINANCIAL INCENTIVES
- Use-value taxation; preferential taxation
- Tax credit for renovation and adaptive reuse
- Smart-growth incentives programs
- Transfer of development rights (TDR)

INFORMATION DISSEMINATION AND PUBLIC AWARENESS
- Hazard disclosure provisions
- Public awareness campaigns
- Right-to-farm laws

Land Use Planning Tools
for Coastal Resilience

Coastal planners have an extensive selection of land use planning tools available to them, including local plans, zoning, coastal setbacks and clustering, and land and property acquisition (see box 7.1).

Local Plans

Many local governments in coastal areas have prepared a comprehensive plan, general plan (as they're called in California), or community land use plan to serve as a template for how a community evolves over time. Community land use plans are a key tool for helping a coastal community to become more resilient, and can and should incorporate natural hazards in the following ways:

- *Mapping* of natural hazards in the community and the extent of people and property at risk
- Mapping of *natural environment features* and green infrastructure that might provide mitigative benefits and enhance resilience
- Identification and *analysis* of population and development *trends* and the extent to which vulnerability is increasing or decreasing in relation to these trends
- Community *goals* and *objectives* (established through a participative community process) for reducing vulnerability and enhancing resilience, and a *vision* for a resilient and sustainable future
- *Policies* for guiding future growth and development away from high-risk locations, and for restoring and protecting the natural environment and green infrastructure
- Identification of *implementation tools* and *measures* for implementing the vision and policies laid out in the plan
- Provisions for *monitoring* and *updating* the plan

In addition to a comprehensive plan (ideally, one that adequately addresses and takes into account coastal hazards), local governments are now required to prepare a hazard mitigation plan (HMP) as a condition for receiving postdisaster hazard mitigation funding under the Disaster Mitigation Act of 2000 (DMA2K). Such plans have been prepared by several of the case study communities profiled later in this book—for example, Worcester County, Maryland (chapter 8), and Palm Beach County, Florida (chapter 10).

In addition, some coastal communities, such as Palm Beach County, have prepared specific postdisaster recovery or redevelopment plans identifying likely rebuilding and postdisaster mitigation opportunities, as well as mechanisms for more effectively guiding redevelopment and long-term recovery. These local plans should be coordinated and mutually reinforcing.

Zoning and Subdivision Ordinances

A community's land use plan typically identifies desired patterns of growth, and zoning and other land use regulations often seek to implement these growth visions. Today almost all coastal communities have some type of land use regulatory capability, often in the form of zoning and subdivision ordinances. Zoning ordinances regulate the location and density of different land uses over time, and may be extremely useful in advancing a more resilient land use and growth pattern in a community. High-risk zones—such as a 100-year floodplain, earthquake fault line, or high-erosion coastal zone—might be reserved for nondevelopment uses or lower-density development that serves to minimize exposure to natural hazard events. Development in natural areas such as wetlands, beaches, and dunes that might undermine their ecological resilience and their provision of natural mitigative benefits might be curtailed or severely restricted. Conversely, zoning could accommodate high growth and greater development density in designated safer areas in the community—usually, though not always, in existing urbanized locations.

Several of the case study communities described in section III provide positive examples of efforts to shift land use patterns to achieve greater community resilience. For instance, the new land use plan of Worcester County, Maryland (chapter 8), seeks to accommodate most of its future growth within or adjacent to existing towns. These towns are located inland and are much less subject to coastal storms, flooding, and long-term sea level rise.

Box 7.2 presents the story of the town of Crisfield, Maryland, which has adopted a comprehensive community plan that seeks to steer future growth away from and outside of the coastal floodplain. Community plans, land use planning, and assorted zoning and other implementation tools, have the potential to guide and steer growth patterns away from the most dangerous locations, and to take into account not only existing short-term risk, but also longer-term sea level rise and flooding. Modifying community land use patterns, and shifting the direction of future growth is potentially a very effective pathway to coastal resilience.

Box 7.2 Crisfield, Maryland: A Community Plan for Coastal Retreat

The small town of Crisfield, Maryland, with a population of about 2,700, lies adjacent to the Chesapeake Bay and faces some stark realities: virtually the entire locality, including its commercial downtown, is located within the 100-year floodplain, and almost all land lies below an elevation of 3 feet (0.9 meter). The prospects for further flooding and the impact of likely future sea level rise have inspired the city to develop and adopt an unusual community comprehensive plan, one that one places flooding and sea level rise at the center and calls for managing future development and growth to minimize long-term exposure to these coastal hazards.

The heart of the plan is a comprehensive land use map and a land use/natural area compatibility chart. The former divides the town into various use zones, while the latter presents an unusual suitability matrix, arranging suitable uses according to how sensitive the land or area is. Land in the city 3.1 feet (0.94 meter) in elevation or higher is indicated as suitable for development, while land lower than 2 feet (0.6 meter) is considered suitable for water-dependent passive recreation and resource conservation uses only. Areas designated as eco-residential are infill sites subject to flooding. Redevelopment here is permissible only "if it restores natural functions and open spaces, links isolated wetlands and natural areas together to provide flood protection and aesthetic benefits, improves infrastructure to benefit living conditions; and provides a broad mix of housing across the affordability range" (City of Crisfield 2007, 38).

The plan recognizes the importance of preserving the extensive coastal marshes that lie to the north and west (including James Island State Park) and to the south. The plan states that these wetlands represent "important resources that protect the City against storm surge and excessive flooding" (p. 29). Consideration of sea level rise and flooding are front and center in this plan. Under the land use map, most of these wetland areas are designated as resource protection and are off-limits to future development.

Perhaps the most interesting element of the plan is the section discussing future expansion and extension of the city. The plan includes an urban growth sustainability area map that indicates specific areas where, through municipal annexation, the city prefers to expand. This preferred future growth area lies completely outside of the 100-year flood zone.

Source: City of Crisfield 2007.

Other Development Regulations

Local resilience can also be enhanced through a variety of other development regulations typically found at the local level. Many coastal communities participate in the National Flood Insurance Program (NFIP) and are as a result required to adopt minimum floodplain management standards (e.g., elevation of buildings, prohibition of development in dangerous floodways). Tree protection ordinances that protect trees of a certain size (and that require compensation when cutting of trees is allowed) are another example, as are restrictions on the extent of impervious cover allowed in new developments (e.g., no more than a designated percentage of land area can be in the form of roadways, parking, or buildings). In both of these cases, performance standards are intended to protect the capacity of the natural environment to function ecologically (e.g., to collect and retain stormwater to cool the environment) and to provide mitigation and resilience services (e.g., retaining floodwaters).

Coastal Setbacks

Many coastal states and localities have adopted minimum oceanfront or shoreline setbacks as tools for reducing vulnerability. For instance, Maui County, Hawaii (profiled in chapter 13), imposes a "fifty-year" coastal setback (i.e., a distance fifty times the annual rate of erosion), with only minor activities or movable structures permitted in the setback zone. Worcester County, Maryland (chapter 8), mandates minimum shoreline buffers along estuarine and riverine shorelines.

Development Clustering

Many communities have also permitted, encouraged, and in some cases mandated, development *clustering*. Here developers are able to shift the permissible density onto only a portion of the development site, protecting or preserving the remainder of the parcel for open space, habitat, or other nondeveloped uses. Clustering gives a landowner or developer the opportunity to avoid especially hazardous portions of a site (e.g., a floodplain or seismic fault zone) or natural elements that offer resilience benefits (e.g., a wetland or forested area) while preserving the market value and development potential of the property.

Land and Property Acquisition

One of the most effective land use management techniques is the acquisition of land and property. Securing public ownership in high-hazard and risky sites in a community means that they are taken off the development market, preventing the future exposure and vulnerability that development would cause. Local governments purchase land to prevent exposure, but also commonly to conserve critical ecosystem or natural features and to provide open space and recreational benefits to the community. Many specific tools and strategies are available to communities for acquiring land, which can be secured either in fee-simple (the full bundle of rights) or in less-than-fee-simple (essentially only the development rights) arrangements.

Financing coastal land acquisition is often quite expensive, given the high value of coastal land for development. Thus "funding for acquisition" is often a significant challenge, and coastal communities have started to look for more creative ways to raise these funds. Local transfer taxes have been used in some coastal states and localities. The Villages at Loreto Bay, profiled in chapter 13, offers another

---

Box 7.3 Maui Coastal Land Trust

The Maui Coastal Land Trust (MCLT) is a 501(c)(3) nonprofit, nonpolitical land conservation organization, formed in 2000. Its stated mission is "to preserve and protect coastal lands in Maui Nui for the benefit of the natural environment and of current and future generations." Formed in response to extensive land development pressures and loss of important beaches and special coastal lands, as of 2007 it had leveraged federal and state funds to buy and preserve more than 1,000 acres on Maui and Molokai islands, In the last several years, much of this protection has occurred in the form of easements negotiated with landowners and developers. Some of the local land trust's funding also comes from local sources, specifically the passage of a county charter amendment, adopted by voters in 2003, that sets aside 1 percent of the county's budget for open-space land acquisition. Like many local land trusts, the Maui trust works very collaboratively in partnership with other conservation groups (e.g., The Nature Conservancy) and increasingly with developers and landowners. The trust's most recent conservation project shows its success at this kind of partnering and at leveraging outside funding. In June 2007, it successfully facilitated the purchase of development rights from a ranch owner on Molokai, protecting through permanent easement some 168 acres of shoreline. In this case, the MCLT partnered with the USDA National Resources Conservation Service, utilizing funding from their Farm and Ranch Lands Protection Program, along with funding from Hawaii's Legacy Land Conservation Program.

The lands included in the trust's portfolio are a former dairy property saved from an impending golf course development, a pristine beachfront portion of a working ranch, and an important shorebird nesting area adjacent to a hotel. In the case of the Maui Coastal Land Trust, the properties acquired and managed usually have a mix of cultural and historic values, recreational potential, and significant natural and habitat values. In addition to the acquisition of land, the trust also undertakes extensive long-term management and restoration work on conservation properties. The trust usually also works to create stewardship endowments that fund the long-term restoration and ecological management of acquired properties.

Like many other local land trusts, the Maui Trust also performs important community education and community-building functions. It has recently organized walking tours of some of its natural areas, for instance, as well as volunteer habitat restoration work days. Community fundraising events are also common, including recently the trust's first Fall Roundup BBQ and Silent Auction (which included, among other things live entertainment and even roping lessons for attendees).

Source: Maui Coastal Land Trust; www.mauicoastallandtrust.org.

interesting and similar approach. A 1 percent tax is imposed on all future sales of homes within the development, with the income flowing to an independent sustainable development foundation, to be used for local sustainability projects (including acquisition, perhaps). This charge applies to all future transactions and thus will generate sustainability revenue in perpetuity.

A coastal community's resource base can itself serve as a creative source for future acquisition funds. For example, a publicly owned community forest in Arcata, California, is managed to allow sustainable harvesting of timber, with the proceeds used at least partly to purchase additional land (Beatley 2005, 154–55). Virginia Beach, Virginia, has for some time been utilizing a tax on cellular phones to fund purchase of development rights in that jurisdiction (Beatley, Brower, and Schwab 2002). Coastal land can also be acquired through land conservation organizations. Thousands of *land trusts* around the country—usually nonprofit, community-based organizations—raise funds to acquire and preserve natural land through a variety of means, including facilitating the donation of scenic and space easements. According to the Land Trust Alliance (n.d.), more than 1,600 land trusts are now in operation around the country. Box 7.3 describes one such example, the Maui Coastal Land Trust (MCLT), which operates in one of the case study localities described in greater detail in chapter 13. Some coastal local governments have also created *land banks* to facilitate this kind of land acquisition. These are usually governmental or quasi-governmental in nature, with a dedicated local source of funding. The Nantucket Island Land Bank in Massachusetts is perhaps the best-known example; it has been successful in preserving about 2,500 acres and, together with other local conservation groups, in securing about 40 percent of the area of Nantucket Island for conservation. The Nantucket Island Land Bank is funded through a 2 percent land transfer tax and is governed by a locally elected land bank commission (Beatley, Brower, and Schwab 2002).

Public Facilities Policy

Decisions about public facilities and facility investments can influence resilient coastal land use in several significant ways. First, these facilities themselves—whether a sewage treatment plant, a peaking power plant, or a road or highway—can be sited and located in ways that reduce direct exposure and vulnerability and ensure that they will be functional following a disaster event. Several of the coastal cases described in section III provide both good and bad examples of this relation to resilience. In many coastal communities, water and wastewater treatment plants are located close to riverfronts and shorelines and are frequently flooded even in modest storm events. In Worcester County, Maryland (chapter 8), these town systems have been located away from and out of the path of floodwaters. Public facilities of this sort can also be designed and engineered to reduce exposure. Roads and highways can be elevated, as can electric boxes, and public structures and facilities can be seismically reinforced and designed to survive earthquake shaking.

Often as critical to a community's resilience is the ability of coastal localities to guide growth through their public facilities policy and decisions. Public investments in sewer and water services, police and fire departments, and roads, highways, and bridges have often been described as "growth shapers" because of the influence they exert in encouraging or discouraging growth in particular locations. The precise tool or mechanism varies, but typically it includes the use of a capital improvements program (CIP) that identifies specific public improvements planned and budgeted over time; urban service boundaries that delimit where investments in urban services and facilities are or are not permitted; and adequate facilities ordinances that stipulate availability of minimum levels of services and facilities before growth is allowed. Some states (notably, Florida) place restrictions on growth-inducing public facility investments in coastal hazard areas. By limiting public investments in or near high-risk coastal hazards areas or resource conservation areas, and by funding or making investments in desired locations (in-town, within existing urbanized areas and away from high-risk zones), a coastal locality can do much to put in motion a more resilient land use and growth pattern.

Taxation and Financial Incentives

Coastal localities can encourage particular land uses and land use patterns through adjustments in taxation policy and by establishing economic and financial incentives (or disincentives to discourage undesirable patterns). Traditionally, many localities have utilized use-value taxation, for example, as a technique to encourage the continuation of farming and agricultural uses. This tool essentially assesses farmland at its use value or agricultural value and not its fair-market (speculative) value, thus reducing the taxation burden on farmers and helping to take away one significant reason why farmers sell their land to developers. The provision of tax benefits (state and local) for renovation and adaptive reuse of historic buildings in the form of income tax credits or reduced property taxation is another potentially useful tool. In some communities that promote smart growth, a more comprehensive package of incentives is made available to encourage development in desired locations. This package typically includes expedited permit review and reduced impact fees or reduced public facility fees, among others.

Many communities use some form of density bonus as an incentive to encourage project amenities or features that address desired public goals or provide significant public benefits. Designs that include mitigation or resilience features beyond what is required by code (e.g., low-impact development features, green rooftops, setting aside of environmentally significant land) might be rewarded in this way. Portland, Oregon, for instance, has adopted an eco-roof density bonus, giving extra allowable density to projects and buildings with green rooftops or eco-roofs (and the higher the percentage of the rooftop covered, the greater the density bonus) (City of Portland n.d.).

Transfer of development rights (TDR), often categorized as an incentive-based approach, is another land use tool available to coastal localities. Here a community designates both conservation sending zones (areas where development is not permitted or is to be discouraged) and receiving zones (where additional development density is permitted by acquiring additional development rights). In this way, unused development rights in conservation areas can be transferred or moved to locations in the community where additional growth is acceptable. The local government can serve as a broker or bank, buying and selling development rights, or serve a more passive role, creating a TDR plan and then leaving transactions to the private marketplace. Once a somewhat radical idea, TDR programs are now in use around the country, many with several decades of positive experience. Notable communities with TDR programs include Collier County, Florida, and Montgomery County, Maryland (see Beatley, Brower, and Schwab 2002).

Education and Public Awareness

Alongside other local land use tools, creative education and awareness-raising tools can be useful in guiding more resilient community land use. Hazard disclosure requirements are now common in many places (e.g., the Alquist-Priolo Act in California, which mandates seismic disclosure, and other coastal hazard disclosure regulations in many coastal states). While not preventing hazardous development, such disclosure mechanisms can at least put coastal property owners, developers, and local officials on notice that future dangers do exist. More general community awareness efforts are also common. Signage indicating when one is entering a coastal hazard area and appropriate evacuation routes (see the examples and discussion of tsunami signage in chapter 9, for instance) can be valuable in raising awareness. Working with particular businesses (e.g., hotels and motels, real estate brokers) and target groups (e.g., schools) in the community for educational purposes makes much sense as well.

Conservation and Restoration of Natural Systems

Hurricane Katrina has stimulated much new appreciation for the natural mitigative value of wetlands and other natural ecosystems. Costanza, Mitsch, and Day (2006) argue that a major focus in rebuilding New Orleans must be on restoring "natural capital"—in particular, the region's coastal wetland system, which provides extensive flood protection and other natural services of high economic value. The economic value of the flood protection services alone provided by these wetlands has been estimated at US$375 per acre per year. A healthy intact wetlands ecosystem would have made all the difference in the world. According to Costanza, Mitch, and Day (2006, 319): "Had the original wetlands been intact and levees in better shape, a substantial portion of the US$100 billion plus damages from this hurricane probably could have been avoided."

In New Orleans, a "Save Our Cypress" campaign is currently under way, created in large part because of the storm protection benefits provided by cypress swamps. According to the Save Our Cypress Campaign *Action Manual* n.d., "Cypress swamps are the best natural storm protection that exists along the Gulf coast, and they are uniquely situated to reduce the impacts of flooding. . . . Approximately every mile of cypress forest reduces the storm surge height by a foot" (0.3 meter). An estimated 800,000 acres of cypress forests remain in Louisiana and are being harvested (in part) for cypress mulch—a practice the campaign strongly opposes and is vigorously trying to discourage through appeal to Wal-Mart, Home Depot, and Lowe's.

One of the most significant challenges for coastal planners today is to find ways to restore and repair coastal ecosystems. Ecosystem restoration can also be an effective approach to advancing regional resilience. One of the increasingly positive examples of such efforts is the new sustainable coastal community of Loreto Bay, Mexico, profiled in chapter 13. The Villages at Loreto Bay is placing much emphasis on restoring the estuary there (fig. 7.1), including replanting native vegetation and mangrove forests that will eventually expand the capability of absorbing floodwaters and provide substantial protection in the face of storms.

FIGURE 7.1

Restoration of coastal ecosystems is an important strategy in enhancing resilience. Shown here is the estuary at Loreto Bay, Mexico, where as part of the development of the sustainable resort project Villages at Loreto Bay, a major effort is under way to repair the hydrological and ecological functioning of this ecosystem. *Photo courtesy of Villages at Loreto Bay.*

Ideally, planners should think in terms of regional systems of green infrastructure—larger patterns and integrated networks of wetlands, forests, and greenspaces that together provide extensive ecological services, including resilience in the face of natural events such as hurricanes and coastal storms. Examples from this book's case studies include the efforts under way in Charleston County, South Carolina, to develop a comprehensive greenbelt in that region (see chapter 11).

Building and Structural Resilience

Determining the resilience of buildings and structures must begin with an idea of what a resilient home or building is, and how it should or might function.

With the emphasis here on coastal hazards, a home or building must be resilient in the face of expected physical forces, such as wind, rain, flooding, or shaking from earthquakes. Resilient design begins with the structural integrity of the structure. Building codes and construction standards are a common and reliable method for ensuring resilience. For instance, the coastal case study community of Worcester

County, Maryland (chapter 8), implements the BOCA (Building Officials and Code Administrators) building code. New construction in California is required to follow the Unified Building Code (UBC), which incorporates extensive standards for seismic safety.

In another effort to strengthen coastal construction, the Institute for Business and Home Safety (IBHS), an insurance industry–funded nonprofit promoting hazard mitigation, has created the *"Fortified . . . for safer living"* (FFSL) program to encourage home builders to build stronger structures and home buyers to seek them out (see box 7.4). Specifically, the IBHS has established additional construction standards, generally above what is required by code, for three hazards: hurricane winds, flooding, and wildfire. Once the IBHS standards are met, the home or structure is awarded a "fortified" certificate, something hopefully valued by home buyers and rewarded in the marketplace. The types of additional building requirements necessary to meet the hurricane winds criteria, for instance, include minimum spacing of studs in exterior walls, use of anchor bolts and hold-down connectors, wrap-over clips for roof connections, and additional roof and truss bracing, among many others (see the *FFSL Builder's Guide* [IBHS 2005]). These standards are intended to ensure that a home is able to withstand stronger coastal wind speeds (110 miles per hour [177 km/hr] fastest mile, or 130 miles per hour [209 km/hr] peak gust).

Building resilience, however, is also a function of the quality of the enforcement and inspection system in place in a locality. Much of the devastation and building damage resulting from Hurricane Andrew in South Florida, for instance, was a function not of the stringency of the code (one of the strongest), but of a generally lax code enforcement system (see Godschalk et al. 1999).

Adoption of a strong code, then, is one necessary element, but adequate and diligent enforcement of that code is equally important. As a direct result of the experiences from Hurricane Andrew, the Insurance Services Office (ISO), in collaboration with IHBS, developed and now implements a Building Code Effectiveness Grading Schedule (BCEGS) that rates communities according to the strength and enforcement of their codes. Communities are judged against a number of criteria and objective measures and are assigned a score of 1 to 10, with 1 being the highest rating. Communities with exemplary ratings are provided a financial reward or incentive in the form of lower insurance rates (e.g., see ISO n.d.).

Increasingly we are coming to understand building resilience in a broader context, and to recognize the value and benefits of structures that reduce demands on

Box 7.4 The Institute for Business and Home Safety

Implementing building practices that better withstand the sometimes violent stresses and shocks imposed by nature is one of the many steps we can take to make our communities more resilient to natural hazards. The Institute for Business and Home Safety (IBHS) is a nonprofit association that engages in "communication, education, engineering, and research" in hopes that their work might reduce the negative social and economic effects of natural disasters.

The Institute for Business and Home Safety's "*Fortified . . . for safer living*" (FFSL) program has been developed to specify construction, design, and landscaping principles that will increase a new home's resistance to natural threats such as earthquakes, hurricanes, tornadoes, wildfires, erosion, and rising sea levels. The FFSL program is distinct from other programs in that it increases "protection to windows and doors, provides better connections between the roof, walls and foundation, and the roof is thicker, stronger, and designed to stay drier." (IBHS n.d.). The FFSL new-home construction designation goes beyond what is required by many local building codes and offers home builders and buyers a variety of options in many readily available and affordable materials, techniques, and technologies that can be applied to a home to make it more resistant to natural hazards. Independent third-party inspections assure that the materials and techniques are used correctly for homes to gain the FFSL designation, which is impartial to techniques and focuses on a variety of performance standards. As many of these upgrades are invisible, the FFSL program and designation need not take away from a home's beauty but rather can be considered an addition to the home's value.

In promoting better building practices in homes and businesses, IBHS supports communities and infrastructure around the nation that locate and build in ways that maximize the safety of citizens and their property. IBHS strives to raise public awareness of natural hazards risk and to supply ideas for how to minimize this risk.

Source: Box prepared by Javier De Castillo, Urban and Environmental Planning, University of Virginia. Information drawn largely from Disaster Safety.org (n.d.).

the environment and that at the same time create more healthful indoor and outdoor living conditions. Homes that significantly reduce energy consumption are by definition more resilient. These individual steps to reduce energy consumption in turn help to reduce the size and vulnerability of energy systems in coastal regions (thereby also helping to reduce the need for additional power plants and transmission lines, all exposed to future natural disasters), and help to create the conditions whereby coastal communities can spring back more easily and quickly from disasters and disruptions. High energy demand, coupled with high storm activity, often results in energy blackouts and service disruptions. Designing homes and buildings that require less energy helps to reduce the impacts and severity of these outcomes.

A number of green building programs and certification systems are now available to coastal communities to encourage these energy and environmental benefits. Among them are the U.S. Green Building Council's Leadership in Energy and Environmental Design (LEED) Home certification; the U.S. Environmental Protection Agency's Energy Star Homes program; and the Greater Atlanta Home Builders Association's EarthCraft House program (see table 7.1).

Hurricane Katrina engendered much discussion of how homes and buildings could be designed to not just fall down or fly apart during a disaster event, but rather to ensure conditions of livability for their occupants following the event. Can buildings be designed to be "survivable" or inhabitable for some decent period of time, and under conditions in which the usual public services and facilities (power, water) have been disrupted? We have already introduced the notion of *passive survivability*, which Alex Wilson (2005) of *Environmental Building News* defines as the "ability of a building to maintain critical life-support conditions for its occupants if services such as power, heating fuel, or water are lost for an extended period." Many of the design elements and building features that would help reach passive survivability are ones that we will need and want to adopt for energy conservation and the other benefits associated with green buildings: passive solar design, and incorporation of natural daylight, natural ventilation, and perhaps more active systems such as rooftop photovoltaic panels that might supply electricity during an extended period of power outages.

One result of designing for passive survivability might be a rediscovery and return to some of the building vernacular and wisdom found around the country. As Alex Wilson (2005) writes:

> There was a reason why homes in the Southeast had wide porches and large roof overhangs 200 years ago, why the New England saltbox had most of its windows on the south, and why homes in the Midwest's tornado belt were so often bermed into the ground. A design criteria of passive survivability would bring back these vernacular styles.

Landscape and Site Design

Many landscape and site-scale features can help to address the urban heat island problem, and to reduce the high temperatures many U.S. coastal cities can expect to face. Green or ecological rooftops, greenwalls, urban tree planting, and use of high-albedo roof materials together could significantly reduce temperatures (e.g.

Table 7.1 Green Building Certification Programs

PROGRAM	LEADERSHIP IN ENERGY AND ENVIRONMENTAL DESIGN (LEED) HOME	ENERGY STAR HOMES	EARTHCRAFT HOUSE
Parent Organization	U.S. Green Building Council (USGBC)	Environmental Protection Agency (EPA) and Department of Energy	Greater Atlanta Home Builders Association (GAHBA), Government, and Industry
Principal Focus	Promotes the design and construction of high performance "green" homes.	Joint program of the EPA and the DOE helping homeowners save money and protect the environment through energy efficient products and practices.	Green building program that serves as a blueprint for healthy, comfortable homes; reduces utility bills; and protects the environment.
Description	A voluntary rating system that awards points to home design and construction that "uses less energy, water, and natural resources; creates less waste; and is healthier and more comfortable for the occupants." Participants reach levels (silver, gold, etc.) depending on points awarded.	A certification program that stresses energy efficiency in building practices, systems, and appliances. Certified homes must meet certain guidelines that make the residence at least 15% more efficient than homes built to the 2004 International Residential Code.	A voluntary program that emphasizes efficiency in building practices and building performance to minimize energy use and environmental impact. EarthCraft provides guidelines as well as resources for builders and developers in the Southeast region of the United States.

Source: Table prepared by Javier De Castillo, Urban and Environmental Planning, University of Virginia, from U.S. Green Building Council (USGBC) n.d.; Greater Atlanta Home Builders Association and Southface n.d.; USEPA n.d.).

see Rosenzweig et al. 2006). While at one time considered an unusual and untested tool in the United States, the use of green rooftops or ecological rooftops has become increasingly common, and many cities such as Chicago and Portland, Oregon, are commonly encouraging them (see Beatley 2005, 124–25).

Many of these same site design features can also drastically reduce the problem of stormwater management, a significant concern in most coastal states. Green rooftops retain stormwater, often as much as 75 percent of what falls on them, and tree planting and other low-impact development (LID) techniques can improve the resilience of the urban environment in responding to rare flood events. Another stormwater management technique is to reduce the extent of impervious cover in a project or neighborhood by limiting paved surfaces, designing shared driveways and roadway space, and utilizing permeable asphalt and pavers that allow percolation of stormwater and the growing of grass and vegetation.

Protecting and preserving as much forest cover and greenery as possible on a site can also be an effective approach to enhancing resilience. A number of hurricane and coastal flood events in recent years have shown decisively the impacts of deforestation. Denuded and deforested hillsides have been implicated in major flooding events in the Caribbean and Latin America, for instance (e.g., Hurricane Mitch in 1998). Forests and forest cover provide many ecological benefits. but one of the most important is retaining rainwater and stabilizing soil and earth.

Good examples now exist of new coastal developments and redevelopments

FIGURE 7.2
New neighborhoods can be designed to enhance resilience by restoring natural features such as trees, reducing the extent of impervious surfaces, and creating conditions that facilitate social connection and interaction among residents, as here in the new neighborhood of Oak Terrace Preserve, a part of the Noisette redevelopment in North Charleston, South Carolina. An ecologically sensitive site plan allowed for the saving of 560 of the original live oak trees on the site, and the homes are subject to design guidelines that require such features as porches and encourage native landscaping. *Photo by Timothy Beatley.*

that seek to preserve and protect the integrity of the vegetation and natural environment on-site. The new Oak Terrace neighborhood under development in North Charleston, South Carolina, is part of the larger Noisette project (see chapter 13). Notably, the vast majority of the site's live oak trees—some 560—have been preserved through sensitive subdivision design and orientation of homes (see fig. 7.2), undoubtedly making the neighborhood more resilient.

At a building and site level, many other steps can be taken to enhance the resilience of a home or neighborhood to expected wind and water. Experience in the South Carolina low country has shown that many specific native species of trees do well in the face of high winds associated with hurricanes (such as Hurricane Hugo). Charleston County distributes advice about which trees have greater wind resistance and thus should be planted near one's home (live oak, sabal palmetto, longleaf pine, southern magnolia, and dogwood, according to the county's Project Impact program) (Charleston County, "Project Impact," n.d.). Vegetated buffers around streams and riparian areas can further protect against floodwaters as well as provide valuable habitat and other ecological benefits. Charleston County refers to these steps as wind-resistant and flood-resistant landscaping (Charleston County, "Hazard Resistant Landscaping," n.d.).

Designing Local Infrastructure and Public Facilities for Resilience

Resilient Lifelines and Critical Facilities

Lifelines are "systems or networks which provide for the circulation of people, goods, services and information, upon which health, safety, comfort, and economic activity depends. Lifelines are the means whereby a community supports its day-to-day activities and include mechanisms used to respond to emergencies" (Johnston, Becker, and Cousins 2006, 40).

Coastal lifelines, then, include community infrastructure providing such essential support systems as water; wastewater collection and treatment; police and fire service; roads, bridges, and transport; communication; and power supply and transmission. Private facilities and buildings that provide essential services—for instance, grocery stores—might also be viewed as community lifelines. "Critical facilities" are also commonly identified, including such places as hospitals, health care facilities, and emergency shelters, among others.

Designing and planning for resilient lifelines and critical facilities suggests several key strategies:

- Designing lifelines like roads and bridges to withstand the range of physical forces expected, and so that they are literally able to "bend, not break";
- Design bridges and highway overpasses to seismic standards that ensure that they will not collapse in the event of an earthquake;
- Elevate new roads and roads being rebuilt following a damaging coastal storm;
- Locating critical facilities outside of high-risk hazard zones, ideally, or in areas of lesser risk, or in areas expected to experience lower-magnitude forces.

Relevant local case studies can be found in section III of this book. For example, Cannon Beach, Oregon (chapter 9), has been gradually taking steps to move its critical facilities outside of its high-risk "local" tsunami inundation area. Worcester County, Maryland (chapter 8), has undertaken an inventory of critical facilities; most, including municipal sewage treatment plants, are well away from floodplains and are located on upland, in-town sites. Ocean City, Maryland (chapter 8), has been gradually placing power and telephone lines underground.

Lifelines and critical facilities in coastal communities can be judged resilient if, in the face of a major disaster or geophysical force:

- Damage to facility is little to none, and service disruption is limited.
- Restoration and return of service and functioning is quick.
- Environmental damages are minimal or nonexistent (e.g., there is no spillage of municipal sewage into waterways, because the treatment plant is located outside the flood zone).

New Ways of Understanding Community Infrastructure

Part of the future challenge for coastal communities and regions will be to profoundly rethink or reconceptualize what infrastructure actually is. The challenge is to understand infrastructure in an *expanded* way (e.g., to include food, ecological services from wetlands, etc.), as well in new and more sustainable ways.

Energy. Instead of reliance on conventional large, centralized coal-burning or nuclear plants with long-distance transmission systems, coastal communities and regions can begin to adopt more resilient kinds of energy infrastructure, including the following:

- Energy-efficient buildings and appliances and land use patterns that require less energy

- Decentralized, neighborhood-based energy production through combined heat and power (CHP) production
- Renewable energy techniques and technologies (e.g., solar photovoltaic and water heating systems, wind, and biomass) that can be integrated into building and neighborhood design
- Tree planting and urban forests, which by their shade and cooling benefits substantially reduce energy consumption

Sewer, Water, and Stormwater. Instead of reliance on conventional treatment and distribution systems, which are usually high energy and chemically intensive as well as vulnerable to disaster damage, coastal communities might begin to see other possibilities for reimagining water-related infrastructure:

- Wetlands and riparian areas provide critical natural stormwater collection and treatment services. Conserving and restoring natural wetlands should be viewed as providing valuable flood retention and as an essential form of coastal infrastructure.
- Low-impact development (LID) techniques emphasize on-site collection and treatment of stormwater. From tree planting to green rooftops and green walls to rain gardens, bioswales, and rain barrels, these small-scale community- and neighborhood-integrated measures can do much to address infrastructural needs and also help avoid high expenditures on large, traditional infrastructural investments.
- Constructed wetlands are an effective alternative approach to sewage treatment.
- Water-conserving plumbing, xeriscaping and water-sensitive landscape design, water-sensitive urban design, double-plumbed water systems, and the like must increasingly be viewed as critical forms of infrastructure in addressing coastal water supply challenges—forms of infrastructure that are of equal or greater value than the usual water treatment and distribution systems and the emphasis on desalinization that can be seen in many coastal regions.

Transport. Instead of viewing transport and mobility in the conventional auto-oriented way, which emphasizes fast movement of people and goods by extensive networks of ever-expanding highways and roads (also vulnerable to damage), coastal communities might consider different approaches to transportation infrastructure:

- Reliance on walking and bicycling should be given equal priority in infrastructure emphasis and investment.
- More investment should be made in transit systems, which are often more resilient in the face of natural disasters (see fig. 7.3). They experience lower

levels of damage, are quicker to restore functioning and service, and have fewer negative environmental impacts.

- Demand management and strategies for reducing travel needs of coastal residents should be seen as a form of coastal infrastructure.
- Design and planning of pedestrian-friendly neighborhoods and communities that allow walking and mobility outside of the car should be viewed as essential mobility infrastructure.

Measuring Coastal Resilience

A key step in moving a community and region toward resilience is to monitor, assess, and gauge the extent to which progress is actually being made. Is the community or region safer and better equipped to respond to and recover from the next natural disaster or impacting event? How do we know this? On the other hand, is the community or region becoming more vulnerable and less resilient over time?

FIGURE 7.3
One measure of community resilience is the extent to which residents can get around without an automobile. In New Orleans, the city's historic system of streetcars provides a form of mobility important to many residents who do not own cars (and who as a result will be less directly affected by future oil supply disruptions). *Photo by Timothy Beatley.*

In addition to developing specific programs, policies, and initiatives to advance resilience, effort should be expended on developing good measures of resilience progress or achievements.

One approach to measuring resilience progress might be to identify specific *resilience milestones*—targeted actions or accomplishments that the community declares its intentions to achieve or meet by a certain date. Resilience progress might be judged in two, three, or even ten years, and according to whether these milestones have or have not been reached (and, perhaps, by how many of them have been achieved). Resilience milestones might include some of the following:

- Preparing and adopting a hazard mitigation plan
- Hiring a resilience officer or staff
- Reaching a certain target percentage (say, 25 percent) of local businesses that have prepared business continuity and hazard recovery plans
- Creating an effective local warning system or other key warning, preparedness, and recovery steps that need to be taken by a specific community (e.g., a broadcast to warn of an impending tsunami, food and material caches located in safe zones)
- Developing a plan and funding source for land acquisition; reaching a targeted acreage of hazardous land in the community to be acquired and set aside from development

Alternatively, or additionally, the community might establish a series of trend- or outcome-based indicators that could be reviewed annually or biennially and against which resilience progress might be judged. Such indicators might include the following:

- Percentage of homes in the community meeting minimum building standards
- Community and regional evacuation times (e.g., in the event of a hurricane)
- Changes in community attitudes toward and personal/family preparedness for natural hazards (e.g., as measured through a community survey in which the same or similar set of standardized questions is employed over time)
- Percentage of homes and development located within hazard zones (e.g., coastal high-hazard zones, 100-year floodplains)
- Acreage of natural land protected and otherwise set aside from development (plus other possible measures of ecosystem health and the resilience services provided by natural lands)
- Extent of damages (public and private) from storms and other natural events over time

Coastal communities committed to becoming more resilient have many different tools available, many of which have been tested by time. No single action, policy, or decision will be enough, and the specific opportunities for change toward greater resilience will vary from locality to locality, region to region. Ideally, what is needed is a package of reinforcing plans and implementation tools, a mix perhaps of the conventional tried-and-true, such as community land use plans, and the new and innovative, such as more resilient small-scale distributed systems for power generation and low-impact development techniques.

Section III
Best Practice in Planning
for Coastal Resilience

What follows is an extensive set of both long and short case studies that together demonstrate the many challenges faced by coastal communities in becoming more resilient, as well as the detailed planning tools and strategies that have been employed. Many of the cases have been identified through an e-mail survey of coastal planning and natural hazard experts. Others have been identified through the literature, and some from the personal knowledge and earlier work by the author. In selecting cases, an effort was made to ensure geographical diversity (with longer cases drawn from the U.S. South, Northwest, and East Coast), as well as diversity in community size, political setting, and types of resilience challenges faced.

The longer, in-depth case studies will provide the reader with a deeper, more extensive understanding of the policy and planning context, the important actors and perspectives involved, and greater detail on the policy and planning tacks taken. The shorter cases, while much less detailed, have largely been chosen because of an especially innovative tool or planning approach, and are as a result more descriptive than analytic.

In-Depth Coastal Resilience Case Studies

Worcester County, Maryland

Cannon Beach, Oregon, and the Northwest Oregon Coast

Palm Beach County, Florida
Charleston County, South Carolina
New Orleans, Louisiana

Coastal Resilience Profiles
La Plata, Maryland
Loreto Bay, Mexico
Kinston, North Carolina
Maui County, Hawaii
Solara, San Diego County, California
Noisette, North Charleston, South Carolina

CHAPTER 8

Worcester County, Maryland

WORCESTER COUNTY IS MARYLAND'S only oceanfront county. It is largely rural but also contains Ocean City, a coastal tourist hub that swells in population during the summer months. The county's permanent population hovers around 50,000 but is projected to reach more than 60,000 by 2020. The seasonal summer population swells to more than 400,000 during peak summer weekends (mostly in Ocean City and Ocean Pines).

The county contains a diversity of habitats and landscapes—40 miles (64 kilometers) of oceanfront, extensive and productive farmland, and 407 miles (655 kilometers) of bay shoreline and extensive wetlands along Chincoteague Bay (Worcester County Department of Recreation and Parks 2006). Assateague Island is also located in Worcester.

Nature of the Hazards

Worcester has experienced significant storm and flood events in the past, though in 127 years of history, the Maryland coast has never experienced a hurricane landfall. There have been a number of nearmisses (with a hurricane coming within 60 miles [96 kilometers] of Ocean City some twenty-six times during this history;

Note: The information for this case study was collected through a site visit and interviews with local officials in March 2007. Special thanks are owed to Katherine Munson of Worcester County.

City of Ocean City 2004). Important nor'easters affecting the county occurred in 1962 and 1992 (Worcester County 2006b). Nor'easters are especially damaging in that they tend to linger for two to three days. Winter storms, such as the 1979 storm that resulted in high winds and 2 feet (0.6 meter) of snow, are also a threat.

A significant amount of property is at risk to flooding and storm damage, especially in Ocean City, the county's most intensively developed stretch of coast (discussed in detail below). Under hurricane simulations such as SLOSH (Sea, Lake and Overland Surges from Hurricanes), category 3 and 4 hurricanes would completely inundate the city, which in 2004 contained almost $4 billion in property value (City of Ocean City 2004, 14). (For a complete explanation of the hurricane intensity ranking system, see www.nhc.noaa.gov/aboutsshs.shtml.)

Resilience Actions and Planning

Worcester County has taken a number of steps to enhance long-term resilience and community sustainability. These include a comprehensive plan that focuses on smart growth away from coastal hazards and avoids development in rural areas and a hazard mitigation plan that takes into account long-term climate change. In addition, the beach resort of Ocean City, the most intensely developed area of the

FIGURE 8.1
The historic town of Berlin is Worcester County, Maryland.

county, has prepared its own hazard mitigation plan and has taken innovative measures to reduce its coastal hazards.

County Comprehensive Development Plan

The county has a relatively new comprehensive plan, adopted in 2006, that takes some impressive new steps in the direction of resilience. The plan projects forward growth for the next twenty years, and then by identifying particular criteria, utilizes geographic information systems (GIS) to identify possible growth areas where the estimated acreage needed for this future growth (3,500 acres, or 1,416 hectares) can be accommodated. In deliberations about growth patterns, coastal hazards were strongly taken into account, and a decision was made to specifically site future growth areas away from the ocean and water's edge, where many assumed growth would otherwise occur. About 60 percent of the projected growth is to occur within (and adjacent to) existing towns and cities in the county (Berlin, Snow Hill, Showell, and Pocomoke) or existing developed areas (such as Ocean Pines). With only 40 percent to occur in new locations, the plan emphasizes the need to strengthen and build onto its existing and historic pattern of growth (figure 8.1).

The county is taking a decidedly smart-growth approach. The encouragement of growth in less hazardous areas, then, is a major thrust of the county's plan, as well as discouraging new growth in rural or agricultural areas. A remarkably impressive distinction can already be seen between the mostly undeveloped rural portion of the county, and its small towns and incorporated areas.

The 2006 Worcester County *Comprehensive Development Plan* clearly states the vision the county's citizens and elected officials have for the future. The plan's main goal, as stated early in the plan,

> is to maintain and improve the county's rural and coastal character, protect its natural resources and ecological functions, accommodate a planned amount of growth served by adequate facilities, improve development's compatibility and aesthetics, continue the county's prosperous economy, and provide for residents' safety and health. (Worcester County 2006a, 7)

The plan seeks to accommodate a projected 18,000 new residents over twenty years, and identifies growth areas where this population will be accommodated. It states the intention of creating these areas "immediately adjacent to or in close proximity to incorporated towns" and anticipates that towns will annex these areas as they are being developed (Worcester County 2006a, 10).

More specific growth area targets, essentially an allocation of the projected population to four town growth areas, are identified in the comprehensive plan. The delineation of actual growth areas was based on an extensive land suitability analysis, described and documented in the plan. The following six criteria were used to identify growth areas (Worcester County 2006a, 14):

1. Contains limited wetlands, hydric soils, floodplains, and contiguous forest
2. Composed of generally larger parcels (100 or more acres) [ca. 40 or more hectares]
3. Located outside of aquifer recharge, source water protection, and other critical areas
4. Situated to be cost-effectively served with adequate public sanitary and other services
5. Located near employment, retailing, and other services;
6. Served by adequate existing roadways (Level of Service C or better) or can be readily served

These areas should have average densities of at least 3.5 dwellings per acre (up to 10 per acre) [3.5 units per 0.4 hectare, up to 4 hectares].

The possibilities and benefits of compact in-town development can be seen in many places in the county. The Walnut Hill neighborhood in the town of Berlin is one example of the kind of town-centered infill growth the county envisions. Here, a 7-acre (2.8-hectare) farm field within the town's borders is being transformed into a small twenty-eight-home neighborhood of green homes only a short walk from the remarkably vibrant historic town center (fig. 8.2). All homes are Energy Star certified and incorporate other green features as well as New Urbanist features such as deep porches and garages behind the homes, demonstrating how careful design and quality construction can achieve many of the goals of "passive survivability" (see box 8.1).

Two critical areas—coastal bays and Chesapeake Bay—are managed in Worcester County. Under the Atlantic Coastal Bays and Chesapeake Bay Critical Area protection programs, an area of regulation and management extends 1,000 feet (ca. 305 meters) "landward of tidal waters and marsh" (Worcester County 2006a, 34). Minimum vegetated buffers are required, and restrictions are placed on impervious surfaces and removal of vegetation.

The comprehensive plan itself has a considerable discussion of natural hazards, especially flooding. It identifies the objectives of limiting development in floodplains, reducing imperviousness, and preserving the biological functions of

FIGURE 8.2
Worcester County has adopted a growth management program that seeks to steer new development into existing historic towns and away from higher-risk shoreline locations. Berlin's new Walnut Hill infill development is only a short walk from the town's historic main center. *Photo by Timothy Beatley.*

floodplains (Worcester County 2006a, 47). The plan also discusses and raises concerns about sea level, stating that "shorelines could retreat by miles in parts of Worcester" during this century. The plan lays out a series of recommendations, including the need to limit new development in floodplains, to acquire properties in floodplains, and to "develop a sea level rise response strategy" that discourages shoreline hardening (pp. 48–49).

The plan also emphasizes the importance of green building and environmentally sensitive design, and strongly states the need for the county to apply these ideas to its own buildings and facilities. The plan has the following to say about energy efficiency and passive solar design:

> The best approach to reducing energy bills is through conservation. An inexpensive and beautiful approach for supplying substitute energy is through passive solar design. Deciduous trees on a building's south side saves summer cooling costs. Strategic vegetation placement can also buffer winter winds. These approaches can reduce heating and cooling costs by more than 30%, thus compounding savings by reducing the mechanical heating and cooling equipment needs. (Worcester County 2006a, 54)

Sustainable building materials, water efficiency, and indoor air pollution are also discussed.

Almost 90 percent of Worcester County is zoned either Agricultural (A1) or Conservation (C1), and the county is understandably proud of its efforts at con-

Box 8.1 Hilltop at Walnut Hill Infill Neighborhood, Berlin, Worcester County, Maryland

LOCATION/SITE

- Infill neighborhood with 3- to 15-minute walk/bike to major grocery store chain, local farmers' market, drug stores, hospital, doctors' offices, medical facilities, dentist, barber shop, post office, banks, schools, restaurants, auto repair and parts store
- Compact community with urban-size lots, narrow tree-lined streets and sidewalks, common open space, cluster mail delivery
- All houses must meet Energy Star residential requirements for energy efficiency by deeded covenants and restrictions
- Home office/apartment above carriage house

STRUCTURE

- Modestly sized 2,100-square-foot (195-square-meter) home with unfinished basement
- Orientation to accept winter sun and summer breezes and facilitate passive heating and cooling
- Minimum north glazing, shaded east and west
- Precast basement walls using 70 percent less concrete than equivalent poured concrete walls
- Framing material of locally sourced yellow pine
- Water-resistant OSB (oriented strand board) sheathing throughout
- No/low-VOC (volatile organic compound) glues, paints, and finishes
- Cementous lap siding
- Reflective steel roof of 95 percent recycled content
- High-efficiency fiberglass windows and doors
- Soy-based spray foam insulation
- Soy-based interior
- Cabinets and built-ins of agricultural waste sheet goods
- Countertops of natural material
- Interior trim of recycled barn lumber and found/saved wood
- Limestone tile, cork, and wood floors

ENERGY/WATER CONSERVATION FEATURES

- Winter passive solar gains / summer sun shading
- Daylighting / natural thermo siphon air circulation
- Supplemental wood heat, mostly from construction waste
- High thermal mass house
- Soy-based spray foam insulation
- Groundwater heat pump with HRV (heat recovery ventilator)
- 80-gallon (0.3 cubic-meter) ambient air stand tank for hot water preheat
- Attic-mounted batch passive solar water heater
- Gas-fired tankless water heater
- Metlund on-demand hot-water circulator system
- Meets USDOE Building America specs (50 percent more efficient than standard home)
- Energy- and water-saving appliances and fixtures
- Dimmable lighting and fluorescents
- Plumbed for graywater and rainwater recovery with storage
- Separate plumbing supply lines to toilets/hose bibs for graywater/rainwater

PREPAREDNESS

- Sheathing glued to frame
- Concrete safe room
- 2 months supply of food/water

Source: Michael Munson, Berlin, MD.

serving these lands. Worcester has some of the most protective agricultural zoning in the state—only five lots may be subdivided from what in 1967 was an entire
parcel of land in the A1 zone. In the C1 zones, this form of subdivision is permitted only by special exception. These regulatory restrictions have allowed the county
to protect its core agricultural areas from sprawl development. The new Worcester County comprehensive plan calls for further strengthening the agricultural zone
and exploring the use of transfer of development rights (TDR). The county has
taken other steps to protect and strengthen farming, including adopting a local
right-to-farm law that limits the extent to which farm use might be considered a
nuisance; it also requires disclosure in real estate purchases that buyers are indeed
buying land in an active agricultural zone.

The county's relatively strong farming sector is another important contributing factor, further discouraging sprawl (it was the farmers themselves who
originally sought the five-parcel rule). Much of the area's farmland produces
corn bought as chicken feed for the area's large Perdue chicken processing plant.
Perdue pays a premium to local producers and has let it be known that it requires
a certain minimum acreage of local production for this relationship to continue,
adding further support for efforts to preserve local farmland.

The county has identified and mapped its agricultural land areas and is making strong efforts to conserve and protect these resources. An area west and south
of Snow Hill has been targeted for land preservation under the Maryland Agricultural Land Preservation Fund (a state program requiring local certification and
provision of state funds for acquisition), and as of March 2006, 4,358 acres (ca.
1,764 hectares) of land had been protected through easements. Worcester has also
been participating in the state's Rural Legacy Program, created under Governor
Paris Glendening's Smart Growth and Neighborhood Conservation Initiative.
Specifically, the Coastal Bays Rural Legacy Area has also been designated, and more
than 12,000 acres (4,856 hectares) have been permanently protected here, with the
goal of another 3,000 to 4,000 acres (1,214–1,619 hectares) over the next ten years
(Worcester County 2006c, 46).

Worcester County has been experiencing a rise in the number of year-round
residents, and an extension of the tourist season in Ocean City (into November
and December). This coastal region, Ocean City in particular, experiences a dramatic seasonal influx of population. Ocean City's year-round population is only
about 8,000 but during the summer it balloons to around 300,000. Fully evacuating this population would be difficult to impossible, and herein lies a dilemma.

Evacuation planners point out the county's limited shelter capacity: the main storm shelters are two schools (a high school and a middle school) that together provide space sufficient for only about 2,000 people. These spaces will quickly fill up, and it would be difficult for county buses to move evacuees to other shelter sites.

In Berlin, a debate is currently underway about whether the town should sell its town-owned electric plant. A peaking power plant, it has in fact kept the town's lights on and provided power when service from the main grid has been severed. Two diesel-powered generators provide the power, and some believe that, given the location of a nearby biodiesel production facility (less than 20 miles, or ca. 32 kilometers, away) fed by soy grown locally and waste cooking oil, the elements of a sustainable energy production triangle exist.

Much of the positive move in the direction of a safer, smarter pattern of growth is attributed to the emergence of a strong environmental ethic on the part of county residents. This ethic in turn is attributed in large part to the good work of the Maryland Coastal Bays Program. One of twenty-nine estuaries designated and funded under the Environmental Protection Agency's National Estuary Program (NEP), the Maryland Coastal Bays Program is a cooperative initiative aimed at studying and better managing activities around the shallow eastern Maryland bays (including Chincoteague Bay and Isle of Wight Bay). Several community-based conservation and education activities and initiatives have resulted from the program (e.g., volunteer water quality monitoring), and the citizenry is much more aware about coastal management issues (Maryland Department of Natural Resources 2004). Residents now realize that coastal environments require stewardship and expect that they will be carefully protected and managed.

There is probably much work left to be done in educating and raising awareness about long term trends such as sea level rise. In making the case for choosing growth areas west and away from the ocean, planning staff brought up the issue of sea level rise, and it appears that these long-term concerns were a serious motivation, as well as a concern about hurricane and coastal storm risks. The recency of the terrible experience of Hurricane Katrina was certainly also a factor.

The county has extensive natural resources and is taking steps to conserve and protect them, such as mapping its *green infrastructure*. This mapped network includes "areas defined by their soils (muck), state-owned natural areas, existing conservation zoning, tidal wetlands and selected riparian corridors" (as quoted in Worcester County Department of Recreation and Parks 2006, 62). (Note: The state of Maryland has also prepared a green infrastructure map for the county, using its own specific methodology; this state map differs from Worcester County's green infrastructure map.)

The county has used various measures and tools to protect these natural areas, including conservation easements; conservation partnerships; implementation of a county Forest Conservation Law; a county Floodplain Management Law; and the Worcester County Critical Areas Program, associated with the Atlantic Coastal Bays Critical Area and the Chesapeake Bay Critical Area.

The Coastal Bays Watershed Conservation and Management Plan has been the main product of the Coastal Bays Program. It represents a comprehensive assessment of the condition and current threats to the bays, and identifies in considerable detail a host of solutions and proposed "actions" to address these threats (Maryland Coastal Bays Program, n.d.).

One identified problem is the lack of recent hurricane activity. The last hurricane to hit the area was in 1995, and much of the county's growth has occurred since then.

County Hazard Mitigation Plan

Worcester County's Hazard Mitigation Plan (Worcester County 2006b) was prepared in September 2006, and has been approved by the Federal Emergency Management Agency (FEMA). The plan is a comprehensive assessment of the hazards faced by the county, current mitigation measures, and proposed future mitigation policies and actions. Chapter III of the plan provides a thorough vulnerability assessment, with particular emphasis on storms and flooding (and to a lesser extent sea level rise, shoreline erosion, wildfires, and tornadoes). The plan provides flood hazard and hurricane hazard maps for the county (100-year floodplain, 500-year floodplain, velocity zone, and hurricane storm surge maps, by hurricane category) and results of HAZUS (**HAZ**ards **U**nited **S**tates) modeling. A review of structures in the 100-year floodplain shows 6,372 structures (including 4,361 single-family homes) at risk, accounting for about $800 million in property value (Worcester County 2006b, 33). As these maps effectively convey, a large portion of the county's eastern edge—oceanfront and bayfront—are subject to extensive flooding, and would be encompassed by surge and inundation from hurricane categories 1–4. The assessment also identifies and maps repetitive-loss properties (properties damaged two or more times in the past ten years), and there are forty-four of these (mostly in the Snug Harbor subdivision).

The county has already adopted several mitigation measures, including a floodplain management ordinance (participation in the National Flood Insurance Program, or NFIP) that mandates a 2-foot (0.6-meter) "freeboard" standard in velocity zones. (Velocity zones, or V-zones, are especially hazardous areas along the shoreline with sufficient characteristics to support a minimum 3-foot (0.9-meter) wave, in addition to flood inundation.) The county also enforces the BOCA (Building Officials and Code Administrators) and CABO (Council of American Building Officials) building codes, as well as wetland setback and buffer requirements. A series of proposed mitigation actions are identified in the plan, with a time frame and priority level given to each.

The hazard mitigation plan identifies and discusses five at-risk populations: children, senior citizens, non-English-speakers, residents with special needs, and low-income residents. A map of median family income is included. Critical facilities are also inventoried and mapped, including "shelters, hospitals and nursing homes, fire and rescue, police, utilities, communication, transportation, and government structures" (Worcester County 2006b, 43). These seem largely to fall within existing historic towns, and largely on higher ground outside of flood hazard areas. Pocomoke's town hall/police department, fire department/emergency medical service, water tower, and sewage treatment plant, for example, are mapped, and located on "upland, intown" sites.

The mitigation plan gives substantial attention to sea level rise (under "less common hazards"), indicating that eastern Atlantic coastlines should expect a rise of between 26 cm (ca. 10 inches) and 55 cm (ca. 22 inches) by 2100 (Worcester County 2006b, 71), and discussing the extent of erosion and inundation that would accompany this rise. The plan also states that sea level rise "requires long range hazard mitigation planning" (p. 66) and ought to be taken into account in future planning and development decisions, though not much more detail is provided about how and to what degree sea level rise will actually be addressed. Other hazards discussed in the plan include shoreline erosion (more than half the county's shoreline is eroding, but most of the erosion is "slight": less than 2 feet, or 0.6 meter, per year; Worcester County 2006b, 72); tornadoes; and wildfires. Existing mitigation policy relating to erosion includes a building setback; a vegetation buffer zone; and, where shoreline protection is needed, use of a nonstructural or "living shoreline" approach is recommended. With respect to wildfire, the plan proposes installing dry hydrants in appropriate locations and mapping potential wildfire sites, as well as educating the public about these hazards.

Chapter VI of the mitigation plan is a capability assessment, and here connections are especially made to the county's comprehensive plan. The mitigation plan states that the 2006 comprehensive plan is "designed to guide and regulate growth and development with an eye on reducing exposure to hazards" (Worcester County 2006b, 84). The plan is to be evaluated every five years, with the county's Department of Emergency Services given primary responsibility for writing and updating the plan.

Ocean City

Ocean City is the area of Worcester County with most intense development. An older beach resort, it is a popular destination for residents from Washington and Baltimore to the west and Delaware and New Jersey to the north. The city occupies a barrier island 10 miles (16 kilometers) long with a total area of 4 square miles (10.4 square kilometers). It has a full-time population of only about 8,000, but its peak summer resident population exceeds 300,000. Much of its development in the last few years has taken the form of condominium units that the city is finding are more infrequently occupied (i.e., they are used only for occasional weekend use or as investment property).

According to Jesse Houston, Ocean City's planning director, while there has been (and continues to be) much redevelopment, the island is mostly built out. Most buildings are capped at five stories through the city's height limitations, with some taller hotels in a few places along the beachfront. The city has prepared its own hazard mitigation plan and has sought to reduce its coastal hazards in several ways. Applying more stringent building elevation requirements is one important method, and the city's code mandates a minimum 16.5-foot (5-meter) elevation for all new buildings along the beach. This is more than a 5-foot (ca. 1.5-meter) freeboard above what the BFE (base flood elevation) would require. A 2-foot (0.6-meter) freeboard is mandated throughout the city, according to planning director Houston. The effects of this elevation can be seen dramatically in some of the city's most recent projects. At the newly opened oceanfront Hilton at 32nd Street and Oceanside, the lobby and arrival floor are reached by walking up steep stairs on the street side, with extensive parking around and under this first habitable floor. One feels above the beach looking out of the lobby to the east. Access to the beach is down a dramatic equally steep set of steps flanked by dunes. Jesse Houston believes this is an effective approach to flooding hazards but describes the streets as a "weak point" in the city's elevation efforts, as it's difficult to elevate them. The city has also designated certain *critical area* zones where stronger building standards are stipulated, including deep foundations and breakaway walls.

Houston tells the story of a recent nor'easter that caused salt buildup on some utility lines, eventually requiring the fire department to rinse them off. Downed overhead lines are a potentially dangerous impediment to evacuation during a storm, and the city has gradually been putting utility lines underground, both through publicly funded projects (the city tries to set aside money in a utility fund for this purpose) and by requiring developers to do so. Whether Ocean City's infrastructure is resilient in other ways is not clear, though. The city has taken such steps as buying backup generators for City Hall and its public safety building.

The city's efforts at beach renourishment are also a major part of the story here. A major renourishment project was completed in 1992, through a combination of federal, state, county, and city funding. A series of nor'easters hit during the project, requiring much additional replacement sand and adding significantly to its cost. Since the completion of the project, the city has to follow a five-year maintenance cycle, with additional volumes of sand being added. The renourished beach system is designed to provide protection for a 100-year storm. A portion of the city's beachfront is also protected by a seawall (with a series of movable locking gates), and on the northern end of the island by reconstructed dunes. The dunes have become quite high, and, ironically, are beginning to obscure visual access to the beach.

Taken together, these Maryland coastal management efforts show serious and significant attempts to plan for and mitigate the hazards and resiliency challenges faced. While it is unclear how Ocean City will ultimately fare in the future (in the face of rising sea levels and increased storm activity), Worcester County's attempt to steer growth and development away from the dangerous coastal edge, and into more inland towns and growth centers is especially commendable. Worcester County stands as one of the few in the United States to have formed a coherent strategy for long-term adaptation to future climate change—one that will likely be successful if it can be implemented

CHAPTER 9

Cannon Beach
and the Northwest
Oregon Coast

LOCATED ABOUT 90 MILES (145 kilometers) west of Portland in Clatsop County, Oregon, Cannon Beach is a charming and relatively small coastal community. With a full-time resident population of only about 1,700, the seasonal number swells to as much as 25,000 on a summer's day. The area is famous for its spectacular and rugged coastline, home to the iconic geological formations of the Haystack and the Needles (fig. 9.1).

Nature of the Hazards

Coastal communities in this part of northwest Oregon face a number of natural hazards, including earthquakes and tsunamis, landslides, flooding, and wildfires. Earthquakes are an especially serious threat to the region. The greatest worry surrounds the 800-mile (1,287-kilometer) fault line known as the Cascadia subduction zone (CSZ), which runs from Victoria, British Columbia, to northern California. Here the Juan de Fuca and North American tectonic plates collide, the former gradually pushing up the latter, with buildup of pressure and potential for a major and wide-impacting earthquake. A magnitude 9.0 subduction zone earthquake event would generate a potentially massive tsunami, as well as a likely shoreline subsidence of 3 to 6 feet

---

NOTE: Much of the information presented in this case was collected though a site visit and interviews with local officials in June 2007. Special thanks are owed to Cannon Beach city manager Rich Mays.

FIGURE 9.1
Haystack Rock, and the beautiful Oregon coast around the city of Cannon Beach.
Photo by Timothy Beatley.

(ca. 0.9–1.8 meters). Geologic studies have shown that the last major tsunami occurred in Cannon Beach in 1700 and that, on average, major tsunamis tend to occur every 350 to 390 years. In addition to these local subduction tsunamis, the coast also experiences "distant" tsunamis originating elsewhere in the Pacific and much smaller in size. The region also is subject to much more frequent shallow (or crustal) and deep (or intraplate) earthquakes on the order of every few decades.

Cannon Beach has made particularly impressive strides in planning for tsunami hazards compared with most other Northwest communities. Much of the city lies within the likely inundation zone for a future tsunami. Cannon Beach's city manager, Rich Mays, estimates that 80 percent or more of the town's taxable property lies within this zone, so the degree of vulnerability is high. A number of town buildings are also subject to earthquake damage, including the city's town hall, built of unreinforced masonry. Five of the six schools in the regional school district are also located in the tsunami inundation zone.

In many other respects Cannon Beach is relatively safe. It experiences winter storms regularly, but loss of power is usually the extent of impacts. The city contains flood hazard areas, including Ecola Creek, which drains on the north side of town, but flooding problems are fairly rare. The wildfire hazard is low, a function of the coastal fog, rain, and relatively high humidity that tend to minimize this threat. Geological hazards exist in the town's higher-slope areas and where special requirements of a geologic hazard overlay zone apply. Coastal erosion and sea level rise are worries. In recent years the Cannon Beach shoreline has actually been accreting, and an extensive and accreting dune system protects much of the city's built environment.

Tsunamis, then, are the main concern and focus of current resilience efforts in Cannon Beach, Clatsop County, and the northwest Oregon coast. Cannon Beach actually experienced a tsunami as a result of the 1964 Alaska earthquake. This tsunami did considerable damage, with floodwaters funneling up Ecola Creek and heavily damaging a bridge crossing the creek.

One of the primary concerns of local officials is that most, or all, of the region will be devastated following a local tsunami, not just Cannon Beach (indeed, much of the coast from British Columbia to California would be affected). While Cannon Beach itself has few bridges, there are a number of bridges to the north and south of the town, and ground shaking, landslides, and liquefaction will likely do considerable damage to Highway 101, the lifeline connecting communities in this area. Any sizable earthquake would likely mean that the Cannon Beach would be in the midst of a region in chaos and destruction, and would be isolated for an unknown period of time. Telecommunications would be out, public services would be nonexistent, and roads, bridges, and airports would be heavily damaged. Cannon Beach officials are planning for the need to take care of survivors for at least three to five days. This means thinking about shelter, food, water, and medical needs, among other concerns.

Resilience Actions and Planning

The city of Cannon Beach has undertaken several key steps in enhancing its long-term resilience in the face of natural hazards. These include impressive work to build community awareness about the tsunami threat, actions to prepare for effective response, and planning to minimize the exposure of people, property, and infrastructure.

Preparing for the Tsunami Threat: Steps Toward Building a Tsunami-Ready City

Cannon Beach has taken a number of steps to begin to plan for a future tsunami, including developing an emergency response plan with specific response directives for staff outlining their duties and assignments under different disaster scenarios. City manager Mays convenes an emergency preparedness committee (including the police chief, building official, fire chief, county health director, and public works foreman) every three weeks to discuss potential hazard reduction steps and planning and to coordinate the city's long-term efforts to prepare for disasters, especially tsunamis. The city and the fire district have also made significant investments in telecommunications: the fire district has recently purchased several satellite phones, for instance, and plans to soon purchase a shortwave radio.

Cannon Beach has made especially good progress in the area of warning and evacuation and in public awareness and education about the tsunami threat. The fire district operates a loudspeaker system that issues a siren alert in the event of an oncoming tsunami (and allows district officials to make announcements and give instructions over the speakers as well). For "local" tsunamis originating from the Cascadia subduction zone, the evacuation time for residents is only about thirty minutes, and extensive signage throughout the city directs residents to high ground. The city recommends that residents walk (not drive) to high ground and directs them to do so whenever they experience an earthquake or hear the siren.

The fire district has taken a novel approach to testing the siren warning system. Its loudspeakers broadcast the sound of a mooing cow as a way of ensuring that residents will understand that a test is under way; the siren is reserved for an actual event. Cannon Beach has had at least one test of this system when it received a tsunami alert in November 2006. Residents responded to the evacuation call, but too many sought to evacuate by car, and a traffic jam ensued. The county is also working on a reverse-911 system that will also likely be helpful in alerting residents to the danger.

Hotel owners have been mixed in their willingness to educate their patrons. The city does not have the power to mandate evacuation, and during the June 2004 tsunami warning it was disheartening to see that some hotels and restaurants were not informing their customers and not evacuating them. In one case, a restaurant manager called a superior for advice about what to do and never received word back in time to do anything. In other cases, the warning was simply ignored by some hotels and restaurants. Some hotels, though, did go door-to-door to alert their guests.

The volunteer fire district offers a program of training and education for hotels and motels, but participation is on a voluntary basis. Fire Chief Cleve Rooper estimates that perhaps one in ten hotels has gone through this training, but, even in those hotels, the high turnover rate among employees means that current staff may not have much knowledge about tsunami threats. The fire district has also offered hotels and motels an Internet-based warning notification system that sends messages directly to hotel desk computers, but, again, only a few hotels have taken advantage of this system.

Some hotels in the area do seem to have gone above and beyond the call in alerting and planning for a tsunami. In Seaside, to the north, for instance, the Microtel Inn and Suites prominently displays information about tsunami threats for its guests. A fairly large placard and map placed inside the hotel entrance shows risk zones, with an arrow indicating the location of the hotel. It would be difficult for a customer to miss this display. However, such hotel efforts seem not to be very common. Much of the preparedness emphasis to date has been on the permanent resident population, and there is some concern this may not be enough.

Nevertheless, the general public awareness of the tsunami threat seems very high. Prominent signage (e.g., "Entering Tsunami Hazard Zone") certainly helps (fig. 9.2). Schools run tsunami evacuation drills regularly, and students study the tsunami hazard in class all the way through high school. Tsunamis have also entered into the local consciousness in other ways, and it is common now

to see the word locally. There is a tsunami bookstore, and a tsunami bar and grill, for instance. One can even find tsunami bark, a kind of local candy, in local fudge stores.

Cannon Beach has also identified two high-elevation locations in the city as staging areas and sites to store and stockpile supplies (food, medicines) that will be needed immediately following a tsunami. The city and the volunteer fire district have agreed to share in the cost of stocking these supply sites over time and have also designated a flat,

FIGURE 9.2
Tsunami warning signs in Cannon Beach warn of this hazard and help to direct residents and visitors to safer, higher ground. *Photo by Timothy Beatley.*

stable site (analyzed by geologists and confirmed as bedrock) where a military-sized helicopter would be able to land during a recovery.

One is impressed with the importance Cannon Beach's public officials have given to planning for a large tsunami. Much of the new emphasis on tsunami resilience comes from the city leadership (especially the city manager and chief of the volunteer fire district) and the enthusiastic support of the town council (one councilman in particular has taken on the issue). The town was also approached by the University of Oregon Hazards Workshop to collaborate on resiliency planning, resulting in a catalytic initial meeting in March 2006 that brought together community stakeholders in a discussion of tsunami threats. This workshop was attended by a number of key stakeholders, including local elected officials, emergency preparedness staff, representatives of the local homebuilders association, representatives of hotel and other local businesses, and public utility and service providers (see Oregon Natural Hazards Workshop 2006). Clearly much is in the works, and tsunami preparedness seems high on the priority list for Cannon Beach.

Seaside, to the north, has been taking similar steps to enhance preparedness and evacuation, with a bit more emphasis on neighborhood-level preparedness and response. It will soon be upgrading its warning and siren system to function more like that of Cannon Beach. Seaside is also working to establish supply caches in safe places outside tsunami hazard zones, and has identified several upland locations where evacuees could meet after an event, indicating these on the town's tsunami evacuation map. Larger areas where tents and temporary housing could be accommodated, and where helicopters might land, have also been identified (several are old logging camps on private forested land).

Seaside has especially made impressive efforts at neighborhood outreach and currently employs a tsunami coordinator. With funding from the National Tsunami Hazard Mitigation program, the city has been working with neighborhoods, schools, and businesses to raise tsunami awareness and to help these groups to prepare for a tsunami event. The city hopes to eventually establish a network of neighborhoods and envisions a kind of block watch program, or "tsunami buddies" program, as one person put it, that would help to prepare and coordinate preparedness efforts at a neighborhood grassroots level. Seaside has been providing a 50 percent cost share for residents who want to purchase a weather radio for their homes, and the Seaside City Council has also adopted an ordinance mandating that every new building in the city must be equipped with such a weather radio. These radios allow for automatic broadcasts of weather and hazard warnings and need only to be left in ready mode.

More Tsunami-Resilient Land Use and Development

While changing land use patterns before a tsunami occurs is understood to be difficult, the city of Cannon Beach has taken steps to move critical facilities and community lifelines out of harm's way. These steps began in the early 1990s, when the city's fire station was moved from its vulnerable downtown location to a location at approximately 40 feet (ca. 12 meters) in elevation, thought at the time to be sufficient to protect it from a local tsunami. In addition to its main fire station, the fire district also maintains a smaller satellite facility, well within the tsunami inundation zone. The fire district is in the process of relocating that facility outside the hazard area and has already purchased a parcel of land for this purpose. Plans are also under way to relocate its main elementary school to a new and safer site.

While the town anticipates the possibility of significant land use changes following a major tsunami, the overall feeling is that relatively little can be done to shape or direct land use and growth before the event, partly because of the limiting geography and land base of the city. Expansion to the east, the only feasible direction, is hampered by the fact that most of this commercially forested land is owned by Weyerhaeuser. The city is negotiating with Weyerhaeuser about acquiring forestland to accommodate some additional public needs and to promote affordable housing, but these forestlands are quite economically valuable (and provide for most residents a welcome greenbelt surrounding the city!). A bond measure is being considered as a means of funding these municipal land acquisitions.

Cannon Beach's land use pattern probably helps in some important resilience dimensions. Its compact urban form means that there is relatively little exurban sprawl into forested areas, where potential wildfire hazards exist (though the wildfire hazard is lower than in dryer coastal localities in southern Oregon or California). The compactness of the city is due to a combination of growth management (Oregon Senate Bill 100 mandates an urban growth boundary with a twenty-year supply of urbanizable land) and land ownership patterns (e.g., the commercial forestland to the east). Under the city's zoning ordinance, forestlands outside the urban growth boundary are mostly in an F-80 zone district, permitting no urban development and requiring a minimum lot size of 80 acres (32 hectares). Cannon Beach's highly walkable environment is one where living without a car is indeed possible, though the city's tourism base is highly car-dependent (there being no other way to travel to or visit the Oregon coast).

The city plans to appoint a "resilience" committee that will be given the charge of exploring post-tsunami redevelopment options. It will specifically explore the town's vision of long-term recovery and redevelopment if and when a large tsunami occurs and the city's downtown is destroyed—for instance, where and how the city might be rebuilt, and how the city might identify these rebuilding locations ahead of time.

The city enforces the state's building code, which is essentially the California Unified Building Code, somewhat modified. This code includes extensive seismic provisions but says nothing specifically about designing for tsunamis. There is some disagreement among experts about the value of strengthening buildings. Many point out that the likely forces of a tsunami are unknown and that the force involved could be so great as to render specialized building elements ineffectual, while some believe that strengthening buildings might at least help in the case of smaller tsunamis originating from far away. One builder in town has recently constructed a home being described as tsunami-proof. The city does have some flood hazard areas and participates in the National Flood Insurance Program (NFIP). It also participates in the program's Community Rating System (CRS) and gets points for going beyond the minimum NFIP requirements.

The town of Seaside has much more extensive and intensive development along the beach, with several high-rise structures and a row of multistory buildings lining the beachfront. The distance from town to safer high ground here is greater. The possibility of vertical evacuation is therefore given much more consideration here, though the city has no official policy relating to such at the moment. As Kevin Cupples, the city's planning director, explains, the type of evacuation needed depends on where one is when an earthquake or tsunami warning happens. If it is not possible to reach high ground in time, Cupples believes the right thing to do is to find refuge in a tall, engineered building. One place he feels may be especially suitable is the five-level engineered downtown parking deck. Cupples wonders if the city should develop and adopt a design standard like that used for seismic shaking—that is, while it may be difficult and costly to ensure the economic sustainability of a structure, at least it should be designed not to fail or fall down in an event, thus allowing it to be used as a last-chance shelter. Seaside is currently the focus of a study by the wave lab at Oregon State University (OSU), which is simulating tsunami impacts on the Seaside waterfront to learn how larger buildings will react to tsunami forces.

As in Cannon Beach, the vast majority of development and people in Seaside are located within the tsunami inundation zone, and the general sense is that changing the basic land use patterns prior to a tsunami event will be difficult. The city is, however, in the midst of analyzing its urban growth boundary and will be adjusting it to accommodate additional land needs, including the possibility of relocating certain critical facilities.

Despite efforts at moving the region's critical facilities in a more resilient direction, many of these facilities will remain vulnerable. The nearest hospital in the region is located in Seaside, and although it is situated outside the tsunami inundation zone, it is vulnerable to seismic shaking. The hospital's renovation just missed the state's stronger seismic design standards (viewed by some at the time as a positive cost-saving outcome) and the hospital did experience significant damage from a minor earthquake in 2002. Oregon's state building code now discourages siting critical facilities within the tsunami zone and mandates a process for siting such facilities outside of these high-risk locations.

Other Resilience Issues

The city of Cannon Beach has also made progress in addressing some of the other resilience issues it faces. The repeated and frequent loss of power has been a concern of the city manager and is apparently the result of downed trees along major power transmission corridors coming into the town. Most of this utility right-of-way is through Weyerhaeuser-owned land, and the city manager is hoping to negotiate the maintenance of a wider corridor to prevent these service problems.

The city is also interested in supporting renewable energy and is exploring the possibilities of developing wind energy within the town. The state of Oregon has been exploring the possibility of wave energy, which is apparently quite promising along the Oregon coast.

Cannon Beach is notable for its efforts to protect its community character and to nurture a unique sense of place (fig. 9.3). The natural setting is spectacular and is clearly beloved by residents and visitors alike. It is a place that is easy to love and that exhibits strong place bonds that may be very useful in cultivating resilience. It is likely that there will be strong desire to do whatever is necessary to ensure that the community continues, no matter what catastrophe and damage occurs.

In an effort to protect its character, Cannon Beach has placed strong limits on signage and prohibits so-called formula food restaurants (you won't find a McDonald's or a Starbucks). And though the homes in this coastal city are indeed expensive, the city's zoning code limits new homes to a size of 3,000 square feet (279 square meters) so there is a scale and "fit" to what is built in the town, and an absence of large McMansions.

FIGURE 9.3
Cannon Beach, Oregon, is a charming coastal town with an emphasis on local stores and restaurants, walkable streets, homes of modest size, and an appreciation for the immense beauty of the beach and coastline. *Photo by Timothy Beatley.*

Cannon Beach has also taken some creative approaches to its infrastructure. It was one of the first to utilize a wetlands-based sewage treatment process, which significantly reduces the intensive use of chemicals. It has secured an upland forested area (known as the watershed reserve), as a major means of protecting (a portion of) the city's water supply.

Resilience Challenges

Although the fire district has a response plan that its chief believes is a good one, he nevertheless worries that road damage and landslides may make it hard to get fire engines and equipment to where they're needed. And loss of water may make fighting postearthquake fires difficult. The many unanswered questions and uncertainties about how a tsunami disaster would unfold represent a significant challenge to achieving any condition of resilience.

Some confusion exists over what level of tsunami inundation is likely or possible, and for what level the city should plan. The original tsunami hazard line established the inundation zone at 40 feet (12 meters) in elevation. More recent modeling suggests the inundation levels would likely be higher. Lack of past knowledge and data is one reason for the uncertainty. In an effort to get a better sense of hazard zonation, the city has helped to finance an ongoing geologic study by a group from Portland State University and the Oregon Department of Geology and Mineral Industries. These scientific uncertainties and differing scientific assumptions have led to differing estimates of risk; some have estimated a 10 to 15 percent likelihood of a large local tsunami in the next fifty years; others have estimated an even more startling 50 percent chance during that same time frame. Either, way the chances are high, and many believe that the region is overdue for such an event.

In addition to the challenges mentioned earlier in getting hotels and restaurants to educate their patrons, local officials have expressed frustration about the traditional emphasis on planning for the first seventy-two hours after a disaster event. This time frame might be appropriate for many types of events, in other geographical settings, but the feeling among many preparedness officials is that along the Oregon coast, planning must assume a much longer response period— a matter of days and weeks, not hours.

The presence of an older population raises questions about how feasible a walking evacuation would be in the case of a local tsunami. In Seaside, even with well-marked maps, an older resident (or even a young resident) might find it difficult to reach high ground in the fifteen to twenty minutes Seaside tells its residents they will likely have for evacuation. An aging population or other populations that may have mobility problems create additional vulnerability. Seaside city planning director Cupples described one elderly couple's solution. Realizing they would not be able to carry much while walking (and it is advised that everyone have with them enough to survive for at least seventy-two hours), they have arranged a small wagon to pull along behind them when the time comes.

Affordability and affordable housing is a final resilience challenge throughout the region, but especially in Cannon Beach. Here the median price of housing is $600,000, making it difficult for city staff and service workers to live within the community. Housing costs affect, for instance, the ability of the fire district (which relies heavily on volunteers) to respond quickly to disaster events and generally presents worries about the social resilience of the region.

Cannon Beach certainly has an awareness of and planning for other hazards, but much energy and emphasis is clearly focused on tsunamis; simultaneously building and maintaining sufficient public concern and vigilance about other important threats is an additional challenge. Sea level rise is a particular concern. Jay Haskins, a local architect and member of city council who has been actively involved in preparedness matters, describes sea level rise as the "slow tsunami," in the sense that much of the built environment is vulnerable to long-term trends in sea level. Sea level rise is on the agenda, but only as an ancillary topic to tsunamis. However, sea level rise is a potentially significant tipping factor in post-tsunami rebuilding scenarios. It would make little sense to rebuild Cannon Beach after a large subduction zone tsunami, even if another would not occur for several hundreds of years, because sea level rise in all likelihood would still jeopardize the town. Nevertheless, there seems little willingness at this time in northwest Oregon to address or plan for sea level rise *on its own.*

CHAPTER 10

Palm Beach County, Florida

PALM BEACH COUNTY IS LOCATED on the Atlantic coast of Florida, north of Miami. It contains the cities of Palm Beach and West Palm Beach, which together were home to a population of 1.25 million people in 2004. The county is a rapidly urbanizing jurisdiction (growing by nearly 10 percent, for instance, between 2000 and 2004). About 40 percent of the county is in highly productive agricultural use (mostly in the west), and much of the eastern portion of the county is highly urbanized, with intensive development along the ocean. Geographically, the county is bounded to the east by the Atlantic Ocean and to the west by Lake Okeechobee. There are extensive wetlands and sensitive lands within the county, including the relatively large Loxahatchee National Wildlife Reserve.

Nature of the Hazards

Few parts of the coastal United States have as serious a threat of hurricanes and coastal storms as southeastern Florida, of which Palm Beach County is a part. More than fifty hurricanes have come within 125 miles (201 kilometers) of the county, with six major hurricane hits between 1900 and 1950 alone. The 1980s and 1990s

NOTE: Much of the information presented in this case was collected through a site visit and interviews with local officials in February 2007. Special thanks are owed to Lorenzo Aghemo, Isaac Hoyos, Rebecca Caldwell, Daniel Bates, and Butch Truesdale.

123

saw a series of hurricanes and tropical storm strikes, including Hurricanes Erin and Irene and Tropical Storm Mitch. The extent of property and people in harm's way continues to rise here, with an estimated $370 billion in insured property in Dade, Broward, and Palm Beach counties combined (Palm Beach County 2004, 3–8).

Resilience Actions and Planning

Palm Beach County has taken a number of steps to enhance long-term resilience and community sustainability. These include an innovative land use planning and growth management system and extensive postdisaster planning.

County Comprehensive Plan

Palm Beach County has been implementing an award-winning and unusual comprehensive plan that lays out its vision for future growth and development. The heart of this plan is contained in its future land use element, which employs a unique managed growth tier map that "defines distinct geographical areas within the County that currently either support or are anticipated to accommodate various types of development patterns and service delivery provisions that, together, allow for a diverse range of lifestyle choices, and livable, sustainable communities" (Palm Beach County 2005, 2). Five distinct growth management tiers are delineated in the plan:

- Urban/suburban
- Exurban
- Rural
- Agricultural reserve
- Glades

Most population and growth is intended to occur within the urban/suburban tier, and, generally speaking, density decreases from tier 1 to tier 5, moving from urban to rural/conservation. The most concerted conservation efforts are aimed at the rural and agricultural reserve tiers, where densities and floor area ratios are lowest, and where certain uses are prohibited (e.g., intensive commercial uses). Reflecting the desire to steer most development into the urban/suburban tier, the plan also delimits an urban service area boundary, indicating those locations where urban-level services and infrastructure will be found. A revitalization and redevelopment overlay zone has also been delineated within the urban/suburban tier and reflects the plan's commitment to promoting infill development within already urbanized areas of the county.

In addition to zoning and land use regulations, the county also utilizes transfer of development rights (TDR) to implement the tier system. Receiving areas are within the urban/suburban tier, and sending zones include rural residential zones in the other management tiers, as well as environmentally sensitive lands. Already significant redevelopment can be seen (for instance, City Place in West Palm Beach) and the value of more compact, land-conserving urban form realized here.

As required under Florida planning law, the county has prepared a coastal management element as part of the plan, and it is here where the most explicit discussion of coastal hazards occurs. Goal 2 of the coastal management element states that it is the goal of the county "to protect human life by limiting public expenditures in areas subject to destruction by natural disasters within the coastal high hazard area, maintaining and implementing a safe and effective emergency management program, and providing for orderly redevelopment in a post-disaster period" (Palm Beach County 2005, 11-CM). Coastal high-hazard areas are defined by the state of Florida to mean those areas that would likely be inundated from a category 1 or 2 hurricane, and a map of these areas is contained in the plan. (For a complete explanation of the hurricane intensity rating system, see www.nhc.noaa.gov/aboutsshs.shtml.) Elaborating on this goal are several strongly stated objectives and policies, including the statement that the county "shall not subsidize new or expanded development in the coastal area" and "shall direct population concentrations away from . . . coastal high hazard areas" (Palm Beach County 2005, 11-CM). Increases in density in these high-hazard areas will not be permitted, according to the plan. Furthermore, for any development proposals within these areas, the county will also review to determine whether they will lead to an increase in hurricane evacuation times and, if so, will require steps to mitigate these increases. Policy 2.1-c says in part: "Developments which cause such an increase shall be required to provide mitigation measures, including but not limited to safe rooms in homes or common facilities, or roadway improvements, such that hurricane evacuation times are not increased in the hurricane vulnerability zone" (Palm Beach County 2005, 11-CM).

Much of the county's resilience effort, however, has occurred through other documents and plans. Few coastal counties in the United States have done as much resilience planning as Palm Beach County has. In addition to its comprehensive plan, the county has also prepared a hazard mitigation plan and a postdisaster redevelopment plan (PDRP).

While Florida localities are required to commit to preparing postdisaster plans, few have actually done so. And Palm Beach County's plan is impressively thorough. The result of a series of public workshops, the document is intended to serve as "a single reference for guiding decision-making and action during the difficult disaster recovery period, as well as detailing actions that can be taken before a disaster strikes to speed the recovery process" (Palm Beach County 2006, iii). The plan establishes a multi-stakeholder executive committee and a series of working groups as the structure for implementing the plan. It identifies a series of postdisaster recovery and redevelopment goals, and then in considerable detail lays out a matrix-based action plan. Proposed actions are divided into predisaster and postdisaster, short-term and long-term. Along with specific action plan items, the responsible working group, jurisdiction involved, time frame, and funding sources are identified.

While the PDRP is comprehensive in its coverage, the emphasis on planning ahead for business recovery and resilience is unusual. Under the goal of "economic vitality," the plan establishes several key objectives relating to the recovery and retention of local businesses (including agriculture and tourism) and utilizing, where possible, local businesses in the recovery contracts. The plan seeks to prevent the relocation of core businesses following a disaster, and to utilize creative measures to reduce the disruption of businesses.

Action plan items include the following:

- Establishing prearranged contracts with local businesses for recovery and redevelopment
- Identifying sites for postdisaster temporary office space
- Securing mobile units that could be utilized as temporary business sites
- Identifying sites for business recovery centers
- Establishing these centers following a disaster
- Assisting small businesses with continuity planning and mutual aid agreements (see Palm Beach County 2006, sec. 4)]

Other business recovery action items include providing bridge loans and (or property tax deferments) to small farmers following a disaster; holding an economic development charrette following a disaster; and, perhaps most importantly, developing special financial incentive packages to "entice" business to remain in the county.

The plan emphasizes actions that can be taken to help local businesses prepare for the inevitable and suggests important steps that could be taken to help develop a more resilient business sector:

Through the Private-Public Network and other business organizations as well at the time of applying for an occupational license, make available templates and other information about how to create a business continuity plan for small businesses. Also, introduce the idea in the business community of mutual aid agreements between businesses. Provide continuity training sessions and presentations at chamber meetings or as special workshops in addition to website and print materials. (Palm Beach County 2006, 4-31, 4-32)

The postdisaster plan identifies a number of other more traditional actions that could enhance county resilience to hurricanes in the long run, including proposals to strengthen its building code (it implements the statewide Florida Building Code but recommends raising the wind speed standard to equal the stronger standard already in use in Broward and Miami-Dade counties to the south); creating voluntary incentive programs for strengthening buildings beyond what the code mandates; reducing the threshold for code compliance for substantially damaged structures (from 50 percent to 45 percent or 40 percent); expanding V-zone regulation to apply to A-zones; creation of a nonconforming structure inventory to speed postdisaster permitting and redevelopment; and utilizing transfer of development rights, land acquisition, and downzoning as mechanisms for moving development out of high-risk locations in the county. The plan also reflects a strong concern with ensuring an adequate stock of postdisaster affordable housing, already a significant and growing problem in this county. It proposes assisting in the formation of community land trusts, and maintaining a vacant-lands inventory that will help in siting temporary housing after a disaster event, among other proposed action items.

CHAPTER 11

Charleston County, South Carolina

CHARLESTON COUNTY INCLUDES THE 100-mile (161-kilometer) coast-line from just north of McClellanville to Edisto Beach to the south and the cities of Charleston and North Charleston. Altogether the county contains a population of about 300,000, and significant population and development growth is occurring in the region.

Nature of the Hazards

Much of Charleston County's population and development growth in recent decades has resulted in the form of urban sprawl. As described in Charleston County's 2004 comprehensive plan:

> Urban sprawl in Charleston County is characterized by a pattern of low-density suburban development that has spread out from the City of Charleston over the past forty years into the once rural lands of the sea islands, the West Ashley area, and the east Cooper area. At the edge of today's urban area, sprawl continues reaching out into the remaining rural areas as development creeps along existing highways, and residential developments continue to appear in an almost random fashion in farm fields. The once rural character continues

---

NOTE: Much of the information presented in this case was collected through a site visit and interviews with local officials in February 2007. Special thanks are owed Kelly Dickson of NOAA, Cathy Haynes of Charleston County, and John Knott of the Noisette Company.

to be lost, replaced in places by fragmented suburban development where there is a diminishing sense of local neighborhoods and the larger community. Rural farmland and forest lands are being lost. Agriculture is declining. And recent scientific studies suggest that urban runoff into the headwaters areas of the tidal creeks is adversely impacting the quality of tidal waters in the Charleston estuary. (Charleston County 2004, 3-2-2)

This historic pattern of low-density sprawl raises many concerns for resilience in the face of hurricanes and other coastal hazards. Evacuation in advance of oncoming storms; the diminishing ability of the landscape to absorb precipitation and floodwaters due to replacement of pervious farms, forests, and wetlands with impervious surfaces; and the social isolation and diminished sense of community that often result from car-dependent patterns are a few of the concerns. The county has taken a number of steps to address these issues, including efforts to contain growth and to protect a greenbelt, as well as a number of steps to more effectively prepare for and respond to future storm and disaster events.

Resilience Actions and Planning

Charleston County's growth and development is guided by its comprehensive plan, most recently updated in 2008. This plan articulates an overall vision for the county, along with more specific goals and objectives for the future. While there is no specific mention of resilience, the plan's Vision section identifies several values and aspirations that come close—for example, protecting the county's unique natural resource base and its diverse regional economy (Charleston County 2008, 15–20).

The plan's Land Use Element gives the clearest articulation of the overall philosophy and spatial vision for how the county would like to grow. Its Future Land Use map delineates an Urban Growth Boundary intended to separate the Urban/Suburban Area from the Rural Area, the two primary land use categories in the county. Specifically, the Urban Growth Boundary is intended to "promote higher intensity growth in the Urban/Suburban Area where adequate infrastructure and services are in place, at the same time allowing for preservation of the rural character of the majority of the County" (p. 28). The plan identifies a number of implementation mechanisms, including the use of intergovernmental agreements.

The Land Use Element further divides the county into more specific future land use categories, laying out density targets and a series of design guidelines to be used in reviewing future development proposals and infrastructure decisions.

One such future use breakdown for the Rural Area is the Resource Management Area, with a density target of one dwelling per 25 acres (about 10 hectares), making this the most restrictive of all the categories.

The plan has no stand-alone chapter on natural hazards and no explicit discussion of resilience, though many of its sections have relevance and implications for resilience. Specifically, the plan's natural resources section does discuss at length the county's abundant wetlands (240,000 acres, or ca. 97,000 hectares—about 40 percent of the county's land area) and floodplains and contains language that supports the protection and conservation of these important natural areas. The plan states that "floodplains are another important natural resource" and that about "sixty to sixty-five percent of the County is in a FEMA flood hazard area" (p. 54). In addition: "Within Charleston County, the storm surge area encompasses most of the major rivers and adjoining estuarine marsh areas. Much of the remaining area that is not subject to storm surge is within the 100-year floodplain as designated by FEMA" (p. 54). Unlike the county's earlier 2004 plan, there is no explicit language stating the county's intention to steer development away from and out of 100-year floodplains.

It is not entirely clear however, whether the county's planning tools and measures have been able to effectively implement its antisprawl goals and its aspirations for a more compact urban form. For one, the county has no jurisdiction over incorporated cities, and, perhaps more important, its land use implementation tools are limited and not necessarily reflective of its goals. Despite the desire to protect farmland, for instance, agricultural zoning regulations still appear to permit low-density suburban development in these areas. The plan suggests the need to explore new implementation tools—for example, more stringent agricultural zoning and transfer of development rights (TDR).

Despite predominant patterns of sprawl throughout much of the region, the city of Charleston has been largely successful at creating the conditions of a compact, walkable, mixed-use city through a combination of strong efforts at historic preservation; investments in urban amenities; and new, sensitively designed and scaled development. The leadership of long-term mayor Joe Riley deserves much of the credit for the renaissance of this southern city. More recently, the city of North Charleston has been the target of new redevelopment activities, especially the Noisette project (see chapter 13), undertaken by local developer John Knott and designed and built around principles of sustainability.

One of the county's more impressive emerging implementation efforts can be seen in the creation of a regional greenbelt. The county's comprehensive greenbelt plan (Charleston County 2006) lays out a vision of a connected network of green areas that will reach 30 percent of the county's area by 2030. This system will also include a 200-mile (322-kilometer) "comprehensive, interconnected system of bicycle, pedestrian, and greenway trails." The greenbelt plan envisions the need to secure and protect an additional 40,000 acres (ca. 16,200 hectares), and a dedicated sales tax was created through referendum in 2004. Actual land acquisition occurs through a rural and urban grants program administered by the county, and a Greenbelt Advisory Board has been formed to guide and plan its implementation.

The greenbelt plan formally adopted by the county in 2006 identifies and prioritizes in detail the different land and habitat types that will ultimately make up the elements of the system. While the plan contains no explicit emphasis on natural hazards or coastal resilience, wetlands are among the targeted components, and the plan acknowledges the important values wetlands have in providing "critical floodwater storage and filtration" (Charleston County 2006). Other greenbelt components include rural greenbelt lands, county Park and Recreation Commission parks, the Francis Marion National Forest, urban greenbelt lands, and greenways. Rural greenbelt lands (those lying outside the delineated Urban Growth Boundary, or area of greatest urbanization) are designated as the largest single component of the future system (41 percent) and may also include marshes and floodplains and other areas that together will help to ensure a resilient coastal ecosystem.

This county greenbelt vision is graphically presented in a concept map that imagines "cities and villages surrounded by green" (Charleston County 2006, 4-3). An example of a "hub and spoke model" of greenspace protection, the concept map identifies proposed trails, current parks and greenspaces that will be connected and extended, cities and villages, and riparian buffers.

The county also continues to operate a very active Project Impact program (originally a national program through FEMA) and funds it through a regular and continuing set of county initiatives. More than 250 local businesses have signed on as partners, a relatively high number compared with other Project Impact communities. The program's main focus has been on education, and it has instituted and supported some creative programs. It has partnered, for instance, with the College of Charleston, and together they have published an earthquake walking tour of Charleston. Other activities of Project Impact include maintaining a speakers bureau on earthquake and other disaster and weather-related issues, developing a scout patch for disaster and weather preparedness issues, and distributing information about wind- and storm-resistant landscaping. A Superior Code home program has also been created to encourage better, stronger construction and renovation practices. Participation in the program is completely voluntary, and homes that follow this stronger code are awarded a bronze door placard announcing that the house is a Superior Code home.

The county also runs the Community Emergency Response Team (CERT) training program. As Cathy Haynes, director of the Emergency Preparedness Division, explains, the CERT program is a recognition that in the event of a major disaster, the staff and agencies to which most citizens would look for assistance will likely be swamped. CERT's goal is therefore to train citizens so they can act as "first responders" in the neighborhood. The idea was first developed by the Los Angeles Fire Department and has since gone national with financial support from the federal Department of Homeland Security. County trainers provide a mix of medical and emergency response training, everything from administering basic first aid to learning how to properly turn off gas and water in a damaged home. As of 2007, four hundred citizens had gone through the CERT classes in the program's first four years. The classes have become very popular and often have a waiting list of eager citizens. The county's commitment to CERT has been significant, with one staff position devoted to the program and many other county staff people donating their time. Perhaps most interesting has been the effort to organize those who have gone through the CERT training. The county has been divided into districts, and CERT trainees are contacted by a district liaison in their home district who continues training efforts after the formal training period has ended.

The county has also been a leader in planning for the inevitable need to address pets during disasters and crises. The Emergency Preparedness Division provides training in disaster animal response and has arranged for use of the North Charleston Coliseum as a pet shelter.

Resilience Challenges

Charleston County learned many lessons from Hurricane Hugo in 1989, and the memory of this event remains vivid. One lesson, Emergency Preparedness director Haynes relates, is the realization that many residents did not have cars and were, as a result, unable to evacuate before the storm. The county now has a transit evacuation system in which Charleston Area Regional Transit Authority (CARTA) transit buses and school buses will pick up residents at seventy-five preset evacuation bus stops and take them to county shelters. The number of pickup stops has been expanding each year as the population of the area grows, but Haynes admits that there are still too few shelters. Still, Charleston County's evacuation transportation plan is unique among coastal communities.

During Hurricane Floyd in 1999, the state did not have a plan in place to reverse the flow on the region's interstate highways; as a result, many people were stuck in traffic for hours, and many fuel-starved cars were abandoned. There is now a written plan to put into motion a flow reversal plan for interstates, triggered by the approach of a category 2 or greater hurricane. (For a complete explanation of the hurricane ranking system, see www.nhc.noaa.gov/aboutsshs.shtml.)

The potential impact and postdisaster chaos of an earthquake is what Cathy Haynes is most concerned about. There is at least some warning from approaching storms, but, with an earthquake, extensive damage to critical infrastructure, such as bridges and overpasses that tie the region together, would likely be a major impediment to reaching people and neighborhoods. Haynes and her division are working on identifying in advance a series of command posts and supply distribution points throughout the region to address this event.

Charleston County can expect considerable future growth and development, and it is not clear whether the county will be able to steer and manage this growth in ways that enhance rather than undermine resilience. There are many reasons, of course, to tackle coastal sprawl: to reduce the fiscal impacts and infrastructure costs of growth; to minimize destruction of open space and natural resources; and to reduce dependence on car travel, among others. Preserving the mitigative qualities of the natural environment through greenspaces and wetlands and strengthening a sense of community and community cohesion are also useful goals that will enhance long-term community resilience. How successful Charleston County's growth management efforts will be remains to be seen, but the county has admirably laid a solid foundation and put forth an attractive vision. It has also taken some noteworthy and creative steps to educate citizens in preparing for future disasters.

CHAPTER 12

New Orleans, Louisiana, and Resilience after Katrina

HURRICANE KATRINA STRUCK THE Louisiana and Mississippi coast on August 29, 2005, causing more than $200 billion in damages and killing over 1,800 people. It was the most costly natural disaster in U.S. history and highlighted the extent to which the U.S. coastline is vulnerable to such massive (yet predictable) natural events.

Nature of the Hazards

New Orleans has been a disaster waiting to happen, and the circumstances of extreme vulnerability to hurricanes and coastal flooding have resulted from a mix of government policy, individual risk-taking, and environmental short-sightedness. Burby (2006, 4) describes well the history of federal support for levee construction, especially following Hurricane Betsy in 1965, and the effects of these investments in allowing, and indeed encouraging, risky urbanization. He notes that "protection of existing development accounted for only 21 percent of the benefits needed to justify the project. An extraordinary 79 percent were to come from new development that would now be feasible with the added protection provided by the improved levee system." Along with federal flood insurance, the levee construction led to massive new urban growth that converted wetlands into houses.

NOTE: Much of the information presented in this case was collected through a site visit and interviews with local officials in January 2007.

Burby refers to this levee-induced growth as the "safe development paradox." In New Orleans, and elsewhere, the "safe development paradox" has been accompanied by the "local government paradox," as the city government has also helped facilitate dangerous development there. (New Orleans' most recent pre-Katrina city plan, Burby tells us, fails to even mention the city's flood hazard).

The Mississippi coastal delta has been losing wetlands at a dramatic rate, through a combination of hydrological changes and ecological alterations. Day et al. (2005) have estimated a total loss of 4,800 square kilometers (1,853 square miles) of coastal lands since the 1930s, and estimate an additional 1,329 square kilometers (513 square miles) loss of wetlands by 2050. The following reasons for these losses have been identified:

- Building of flood control levees
- Closing of most active tributaries, and dredging of river mouth, resulting in "loss of most river sediments, which once sustained the wetlands, directly to deep waters of the Gulf of Mexico" (p. 255)
- Dam construction in the upper Mississippi River, resulting in a reduction of suspended sediment
- Extensive dredging of canals for drilling access, pipeline canals, deep-draft navigation channels (an estimated 15,000 kilometers, or 9,320 miles, of canals in wetlands)

Much study of the Mississippi delta ecosystem has been done, and some bold ecosystem restoration plans have been formulated. Coast 2050, and most recently the Louisiana Coastal Area (LCA) Ecosystem Restoration Study, lay out a vision of a restored ecosystem and a number of specific actions and projects that would help to bring about this restoration (U.S. Army Corps of Engineers 2004). The LCA Ecosystem Study, prepared by U.S. Army Corps of Engineers and incorporating the findings of Coast 2050, identifies key near-term "critical restoration features," including flow diversions, bayou reintroductions, and shoreline restoration work. Some of these are recommended for implementation, others for further study.

Resilience Actions and Planning

Restoring and repairing the region's natural systems and ecology would do much to build resilience. Costanza, Mitsch, and Day (2006, 319) recommend converting areas below sea level back to wetlands or allowing only buildings that are able to adapt to occasional flooding conditions; rebuilding wetland systems outside of the levees as flood protection; restoring much of the natural flow and functioning of the Mississippi River; rebuilding the social capital of the city; and viewing the city's renewal and rebuilding as a way of demonstrating what a future sustainable city could look like:

> We should restore the built capital of New Orleans to the highest standards of high-performance green buildings and a car-limited urban environment with high mobility for everyone. New Orleans has abundant renewable energy sources in solar, wind, and water. What better message than to build a 21st-century sustainable city running on renewable energy on the rubble of a 20th-century oil and gas production hub. In other words, New Orleans should be built higher, stronger, much more efficient, and designed to make extensive use of renewable energy. One can imagine a new pattern for the residential neighborhoods of New Orleans with strong, multistory, multifamily buildings surrounded by green space, each with enough water and fuel storage for several weeks, operating principally on wind and solar energy.

Much of the discussion on rebuilding has centered around the question of how to provide adequate (and often short term) housing for those who have been displaced. The emergence of Federal Emergency Management Agency (FEMA) trailer-villes has been a disturbing development and has led some to search for alternatives to putting families in such trailers for long periods of time. The so-called Katrina Cottages were developed as an alternative approach to this problem. More substantial and designed by architects, but about the same size as a trailer, these cottages are viewed as a much more acceptable way to house families for extended periods of time.

One obstacle to using Katrina Cottages is that FEMA has been unable to fund them as an alternative. The agency feels it is restricted from funding them because, under the Stafford Act, Katrina Cottages would not be considered temporary housing, and FEMA cannot fund "permanent" housing. Mayor Connie Moran of Ocean Springs, Mississippi, has been a big proponent of the cottages and would like to see Congress change the law to grant funding for their purchase.

If communities were able to fund and build Katrina Cottages, these cottages would provide short-term housing and would also add to the stock of permanent housing in a community, and would on many levels probably be more sustainable housing than trailers. As New Orleans mayor Ray Nagin notes: "How much sense does it make to invest millions upon millions of dollars into FEMA travel trailers that are only going to end up on the trash heap in a couple of years?" (Norris 2006).

In addition, new revelations suggest that living in these trailers may be profoundly unhealthy. As many as 120,000 households lived in FEMA trailers at the peak, and even today some 66,000 families continue to live in them (Hsu 2007, A8). Tests suggest, however, high levels of formaldehyde off-gassing in the trailers, as high as seventy-five times the federal health standards. FEMA apparently knew of this problem but failed to engage systemic testing for fear of liability (see Hsu 2007). Few would expect or advocate that large numbers of people remain living in trailers for long periods of time. Thus postdisaster housing—the difficulty in providing it and the need for better, more creative, and healthier options—has become a major lesson following Katrina.

How and in what ways the city and region should rebuild have, of course, been major topics of study and analysis, and a number of different rebuilding and recovery plans have been issued by various government and nongovernmental organizations. The Urban Land Institute (ULI), for instance, assembled its own visiting team and issued a recommended rebuilding plan called the Bring Back New Orleans Plan. The U.S. Green Building Council (USGBC) convened a multi-day design charrette, and prepared its own green plan for rebuilding. Presented as a series of ten principles, called the New Orleans Principles, they propose a variety of ambitions and innovative green ideas from reforesting the city to expanding transit to neighborhood schools (these principles can be found in chapter six). The plan and principles call for smart redevelopment, with higher density mixed-use centers in safer locations in the city.

The Unified New Orleans Plan, a "broad-based citizen planning process" funded through the Greater New Orleans Foundation, has resulted in the development of a Citywide Strategic Recovery and Building Plan. This plan integrates the earlier plans; provides a detailed recovery assessment (hurricane impacts, population trends, future flooding risks, etc.); lays out a "recovery vision" and recovery goals; and provides a detailed set of recovery projects and programs intended to meet these goals and vision. The latter is extremely comprehensive, addressing flood protection, transportation, housing, community services, historic preservation, and urban design, among others (see City of New Orleans 2006).

The latest chapter in the rebuilding efforts and vision for the city of New Orleans is a new redevelopment plan unveiled in the spring of 2007 by the city's new director of the Office of Recovery Management, Ed Blakely, a respected academic and planner. The plan identifies seventeen targeted redevelopment areas spread throughout the city, each about 0.5 mile (0.8 kilometer) in diameter. These areas are envisioned as catalysts for development and will be where public and private investment will be focused. The cost of this plan, $1.1 billion, makes it much less ambitious (and more realistic to many observers) than previous plans. It will be funded through a combination of bonds with the hope that the federal government will relieve the city of its 10 percent share of disaster assistance funds (an exception made following 9/11 and other disasters, so some precedence exists). Interestingly, these redevelopment zones are centered on the historic location of the city's old markets, which used to be the centers of neighborhood life. And while one of the zones includes the Lower Ninth Ward,

FIGURE 12.1
The first Global Green House and an early rendering of Global Green's Holy Cross Project in New Orleans' Lower Ninth Ward reflect principles of sustainability and resilience.
Photo by Lever Rukhin. Early rendering by workshop/apd.

some fourteen of the seventeen are sited in the less flooded western areas of the city (see, e.g., Nossiter 2007a, 2007b).

Many of the organizations and agencies involved in rebuilding activities in New Orleans have been advancing a "green agenda." This new "green building" includes a project supported by the Enterprise Foundation to rebuild the Lafitte public housing project, based on their Green Communities green design criteria. Global Green USA has just completed the first homes in its Holy Cross Project, a mixed-use development in the Holy Cross neighborhood in the Lower Ninth Ward with major funding from the Home Depot Foundation (see fig. 12.1). Brad Pitt's Make It Right Foundation is also working on a larger green project that will eventually provide some 150 green homes, also in the struggling Lower Ninth. This project has already generated some creative new designs for affordable green houses, including a number of resilience features (elevated homes, solar panels, escape hatches), and has employed visionary green designer William McDonough. Pitt has already raised money to build more than 90 of these homes.

According to Walker Wells (pers. comm.), who runs the Green Urbanism Program at Global Green USA, the Holy Cross houses and project will also incorporate some key resilience features:

- They are located on high ground close to the river and levee, which is about 6 feet (1.8 meters) above sea level.
- A pier foundation system addresses weak soils and possible lifting from the foundation due to buoyancy during flooding.
- The first floor is elevated another 3 feet (0.9 meter) above grade.
- Rigid foam insulation is used that is less easily damaged by water and dries out more quickly.
- Insulation is placed on the exterior between the sheathing and siding so, if necessary, it can replaced without damage to the interior.
- Paperless drywall is used on the ground floor to preclude or limit mold growth.
- Mechanical equipment and the electrical switch box are placed on the second floor to reduce risk of water damage.
- Windows and solar panels are rated to withstand impact from hurricane-force winds.

The first of the Holy Cross homes has been completed, according to Wells, and has received Platinum certification under the U.S. Green Building Council's LEED certification process. Work was begun on the next two homes in early 2009, and there are plans to seek certification for the entire development under USGBC's LEED-ND (Neighborhood Development) program.

Resilience Challenges

Following Hurricane Katrina, much of the city's population relocated to other cities, and New Orleans' current population is still less than half what it was pre-Katrina. Many demographers and economists are not surprised; they believe that the social ills of New Orleans—very high levels of unemployment and poverty, a high crime rate, and what one recent observer described as a "basket case" economy—suggest the merits of a poststorm population readjustment. These prestorm conditions, moreover, illustrate the high degree of social vulnerability that existed in this coastal city.

The inability of many residents to evacuate (there is no viable mass transit system, and some 25 percent of the city's residents did not own automobiles), coupled with the city's inadequate plans for transporting these residents out of harm's way, has become a major issue. Significant efforts have been made during the last two hurricane seasons to arrange bus and train transportation in the event of another storm evacuation (though not without logistical and planning difficulties). Katrina demonstrated vividly the vulnerability of urban coastal populations and coastal cities that have few nonauto transportation options.

Hurricane Katrina has highlighted other significant ways in which New Orleans' population is vulnerable, with lessons for other major coastal cities. Food availability and food security have emerged as significant concerns; even today, many grocery stores have not reopened in the city, and those that have reopened require a car to reach them. Immediately following the hurricane, a coalition of organizations called the New Orleans Food and Agriculture Network prepared a New Orleans Food Map to assist residents in locating food in the city. This map has been updated and placed on the Web (see www.nolafoodmap.com), and is being used as a kind of diagnostic tool for food planning in the city. Moving the city and its residents in the direction of greater food security has taken a number of tacks, including work to reactivate several community farmers' markets in the city and to incorporate food production and education into city schools. Schools became a major source of food, indeed the major source, for many children in the city. A pilot effort to incorporate a garden and food production has been under way in one school—Green Elementary—with the help and sponsorship of Alice Waters, who started the Edible Schoolyard program in California. Kids at Green Elementary are already growing some produce, and a large food-producing garden is envisioned.

Despite New Orleans' long and distinguished food and cooking heritage, it is interesting that there is so little connection with local food and so many food security challenges. At one point in the city's history, as recently as the 1950s, there were some thirty-four publicly owned markets, which were the lifeblood of communities and neighborhoods. These are all gone at this point. There are no functioning CSAs ("community-supported agriculture," a kind of subscription farming) in the city, and, with the exception of several small and temporary farmers' markets, there is relatively little direct connection between local and regional producers and consumers. A food policy council has, however, been proposed, and the food vulnerabilities and insecurities uncovered by Katrina will likely need to be further addressed in the future.

But there are hopeful signs nonetheless. A number of prominent restaurants in the city have now rekindled what ideally will be long-term relationships with area growers. These connections are good for resilience and sustainability and, from the restaurant's point of view, provide considerable benefits in terms of taste, freshness, and health.

Hurricane Katrina was a devastating event for New Orleans, but if there is any silver lining to the disaster, it is that the impacts and difficult recovery have served to highlight the many ways in which many other coastal cities are not resilient. Profound inequalities related to income and race were brought out in the patterns of vulnerability and the impacts of the storm, as well as ineffective and inadequate federal disaster response, severe difficulties in rebuilding and stimulating the recovery of this historic city, and ongoing struggles to return it to its earlier population and economy. Yet there have been a number of new resilience ideas, innovative planning efforts, and pilot initiatives that have arisen from the circumstances of New Orleans. These include, for instance, the concept of passive survivability (discussed extensively in chapter 6) and new ideas for building green and resilient buildings and neighborhoods. And while the story of New Orleans is still being written, the city may in the end bounce back and become a model of future resilience and sustainability. Whatever happens, New Orleans will serve as a cautionary tale, a visceral and moving testament to the vulnerabilities of coastal life signaling an urgent need to confront the serious issues of coastal resilience faced up and down the U.S. coastline.

CHAPTER 13

Brief Coastal Resilience Profiles

THERE ARE MANY POSITIVE STORIES to tell about coastal communities that have made significant strides and have undertaken interesting and innovative measures to become more resilient. What follows is a series of shorter cases that together provide additional insights and ideas about what is possible. Identified through the literature and through consultation with leading national experts in coastal management, they vary geographically from Hawaii to California to South Carolina. They vary as well in the types of strategies and tools they have employed. Together these briefer cases provide a cross-section of the good coastal practice under way around the country.

La Plata, Maryland: Rebuilding after a Devastating Tornado

A fierce tornado (F4) barreled through the center of the small town of La Plata on Sunday evening, April 28, 2002. Damage was extensive, though loss of life (four) and injury were remarkably small. The town considers itself lucky in that the path managed to avoid (barely) a major senior living facility, as well as the city's hospital. Also, because the tornado occurred on a Sunday, no students died in the Archbishop Neale Elementary School, which was obliterated by the force of the storm.

Damage to the town's building stock, however, was considerable. About forty-eight businesses and forty-one homes were destroyed by the tornado, and more than $100 million in damages resulted overall. The storm also destroyed some five thousand trees in Charles County in a swath that was more than 20 miles (32 kilometers) long and nearly half a mile (0.8 kilometer) wide. This was a fast-moving tornado, traveling through the town at nearly 60 miles per hour (96 kilometers per hour). The actual destruction took only about forty seconds.

La Plata and its leaders saw the tornado as an opportunity to rebuild better and to remake the town in some important ways. The clearest lesson from the La Plata story is the value of having a plan, a long-term vision that can be used to guide rebuilding and redevelopment. To the town's credit, it had been thinking about this issue for some time, having gone through a community visioning process and preparation of a new downtown plan over roughly a five-year period. This plan was originally envisioned to apply to the former industrial areas on the north end of the downtown, but following the devastating tornado, the plan was quickly shifted to those parts of the downtown that would now confront rebuilding.

The new downtown plan envisioned growing in quite different ways, promoting new development that would be pedestrian-friendly and encourage mixed use, with residences above businesses. The town's vision for the future was modeled after Annapolis or Ellicott City (both historic Maryland cities, very compact and walkable). More people living downtown is part of this vision, and the replacing of single-story structures with multistory buildings along tree-lined, attractive, and walkable streets. As then-mayor William Eckman (quoted in Ridge 2003) explains: "When I first moved here 33 years ago, there were three places on Charles Street to buy a suit. . . . Now you can't even find a handkerchief. The goal is to have more people living downtown, more shops, and get people to come here, park their cars and walk from place to place."

Following the tornado, the town was able to put in place significant financial incentives to property owners willing to rebuild according to the design standards and town vision. Specifically, up to $25,000 of the costs of the rebuilding would be covered by the town, through funds received from the state. In many respects, it does appear that La Plata is rebuilding in a smarter way. Reconstruction has occurred on most of the destroyed sites, often replacing a modest building with something larger and more substantial. And while the downtown has lost several businesses, most want to stay, and many have taken advantage of the incentive grants provided. Many of the new buildings on LaGrange Avenue, a street hard hit by the tornado, are building consistent with the new town vision.

La Plata also demonstrates, as city manager Doug Miller is quick to point out, the importance of being adequately prepared for such an event on a number of levels. La Plata was not, he will tell you. The town lacked an adequate hardened space (i.e., a structurally reinforced building that could better withstand storm forces) from which to operate, and the town hall had no emergency generator. Miller's twelve-hour-telephone-battery system was inadequate for communications following the disaster. It took two hours to shut the water valve to stop the hemorrhaging of water following the collapse of one of the town's four water towers. The town had no mutual-aid agreements and was overwhelmed by the debris and recovery crisis it faced. Yet the response from other local jurisdictions was heartening. Crews and personnel arrived from many sister jurisdictions, from Ocean City, Montgomery County, Baltimore, and the District of Columbia. However, the town discovered one significant implication of having no formal mutual-aid agreements—the Federal Emergency Management Agency (FEMA) refused to reimburse for expenses incurred by these crews and personnel from other jurisdictions.

A remarkable part of the story is the energy and goodwill provided by residents in the aftermath of the tornado, and the extent of personal initiative and responsibility taken by many. These residents are what city manager Miller calls the local "heroes." One business couple, Lisa and Paul Bales, made their restaurant, the Crossing at Casey Jones, the central meeting stop for downtown business. Two days after the storm, this restaurant was the site of a cathartic community meeting. Another local businessman, Paul Facchina, took it upon himself to clear a parcel of land downtown and to install temporary trailers to accommodate businesses affected by the tornado. Many have reinvested in the town, like Marty Martin's grand rebuilding of his gas station (complete with brick columns).

La Plata could suffer from another kind of hazard, as a major floodplain runs near downtown. However, the floodplain has been mostly protected in old-growth woodlands, thanks to stronger floodplain regulations in Maryland, as well as forward-looking property owners. The town envisions acquiring some of this land, and views it as necessary to protect a contiguous habitat here. The extensive residential development occurring around La Plata may be able to contribute to this land acquisition through the state's forest mitigation standards. Where existing trees and woodlands are destroyed, developers must mitigate or compensate, and protecting woodlands in this floodplain may be encouraged in the future.

Another lesson from La Plata is the need to commemorate, celebrate, and give thanks. For the one-year anniversary of the tornado, the town held a three-day Celebrate La Plata festival, a time to remember the somber event, but also to have fun and to mark the rebirth of this resilient town.

The Villages at Loreto Bay, Baja California Sur: A Model of a New, Resilient, and Sustainable Coastal Town

Purporting to be the largest sustainable development in North America, a new coastal resort community, the Villages at Loreto Bay, on the Sea of Cortez in Baja California Sur, Mexico, is offering an impressive model for future resilient and sustainable coastal development. A $3 billion community on a 8,000-acre (ca. 3,200-hectare) site, the Villages at Loreto Bay will eventually contain 6,000 homes, essentially creating a new, sustainably designed coastal town.

From the beginning, this large project has taken a different path, one in which long-term sustainability is at the center. Specifically, the project has been designed as a series of nine compact, car-free villages where residents will get around by walking, biking, or electric carts. All homes are designed to be energy-efficient, utilizing passive solar energy and solar water heating. The courtyard homes utilize local materials such as local stone where possible, and native landscaping is used throughout the project. At the landscape level, 5,000 of the 8,000 acres (ca. 2,000 of the 3,200 hectares) will be set aside as a nature preserve and areas of habitat restoration.

Particular attention in Loreto Bay is given to energy, water, and biodiversity. The project is underwriting a 20-megawatt wind farm that will produce more energy than the community will need, and the homes are being designed to reduce their energy needs from the start: inner courtyards, fountains, and domed vented kitchen cupolas will help to naturally cool the homes (fig. 13.1). The above-kitchen cupolas serve as solar pumps, pulling heat up and drawing in cool air from the courtyards to ground level. Courtyards contain fountains that provide further cooling benefits. Together these features add up to what David Butterfield (former chairman of the Loreto Bay Company and a driving force behind the project) calls a "living house" that "cools itself." Homes are clustered together to further reduce energy consumption and to moderate climate, with the common areas between the homes used to collect and capture stormwater runoff.

The Villages at Loreto Bay have been designed around the principles of New

Urbanism, including narrow streets and walkable, mixed-use environments, but, instead of porches, each home has a roof deck that serves a similar function. The developer envisions that much rooftop food production could occur, as the climate allows the growing of just about any tropical fruit or food. Edible plants and landscaping will be encouraged and assisted, so that "every homeowner can have food growing."

A similar approach is being taken to reduce water usage through water landscaping (the paspalum grass used on the golf course is saline-tolerant and needs little water, thus reducing the need for fungicides and herbicides); collecting and harvesting more water than is needed; and reusing wastewater for landscaping, irri-

FIGURE 13.1
The homes at the Villages at Loreto Bay are green and sustainable. Designed to utilize natural ventilation and cooling, and local materials and craftsmen, they also include unusual features such as rooftop terraces. *Photos courtesy of the Villages at Loreto Bay.*

gation, and farming. The goal is to add to, rather than diminish, biodiversity by working to revegetate and restore the estuary and wetlands systems. including the planting of thousands of mangroves.

The development has also been organized from the beginning to utilize local materials and labor as much as possible. Local craftsman are employed to build the homes in the community, and a 25-acre (10-hectare) organic farm will produce much of the food needed for the community. The emphasis on local building materials in the early phase of production—especially locally made compressed earthen blocks—was especially impressive, and David Butterfield has estimated that some 90 percent of the mass of the building occurring in the first phases has come from within 1 mile (1.6 kilometers) of the community.

Some of the original home building materials have changed, however—for example, the project has stopped using the locally made compressed earthen blocks. A story in the evolution of sustainable building practices, the experiences with the bricks during summer months found that they kept the home too hot and significantly raised air-conditioning bills. In addition, they were highly labor-intensive, resulting in increased costs for the homes. The importation of workers to make the blocks also create social sustainability issues as housing outside workers became a serious concern. The developers have now shifted to a new building material and system called PermaWall, which has its own interesting sustainability story. These premade building panels, constructed in Mexicali on the Mexican mainland, utilize in part recycled Styrofoam from packing containers from a take-back initiative. The PermaWall system has been found to provide better insulation value and does a better job of maintaining cool temperatures (and thus reducing peak electricity loads) during the summer.

Other important sustainability features include an impressive recycling of 75 percent of the construction waste, planned composting of all organic waste, and use of Energy Star appliances and low-VOC paints and finishes, among others. All new homes are equipped with solar water heating. Dark sky lighting is also being used.

The Inn at Loreto Bay is also an important sustainability story. This 155-room hotel incorporates a number of green features in its operation and has recently received a bronze certification level from the international organization Green Globe. Green features include low-energy lighting, use of organic and local food, waste reduction and recycling efforts, and use of native plants and landscaping, among others. The hotel has even shifted to using recyclable cardboard key cards. Most interesting are the ecotourism programs offered to guests (e.g., turtle watching, whale watching, hikes to important historic sites) and the opportunities guests have to volunteer locally (e.g., working with local schools on an "edible schoolyard" program).

Peter Clark, the development's sustainability director, has been somewhat (pleasantly) surprised at how effective the basic urban form of the village has been in facilitating social interaction and nurturing friendships among the early residents of the neighborhood. The tenets of New Urbanism have proved to work here, according to Clark, who has witnessed the development of close friendships, the building of a real sense of community, and the engagement of residents in the life of Loreto Bay. The process for selling the homes is unusual and helps to create community from the beginning. The Loreto Bay Company sells homes only eight days a year, and potential buyers visit and learn about the development together in groups of one hundred to two hundred. People interact and socialize (culminating in a dance on the last night) and begin the process of getting to know at least some of the people who will become their neighbors. Social sustainability and commitment to the local community are advanced in other ways as well. One percent of the sale of each home goes to the Loreto Bay Foundation, an organization independent of the developer, with the funds used to finance sustainability projects in and around the town of Loreto. This 1 percent charge will apply to all future real estate transactions in perpetuity, so a steady stream of community funding is created through this mechanism. Sales have already generated $3 million for the foundation, which has pledged to support a variety of worthy local projects (e.g., a new hospital, a youth soccer league, and a new environmental center).

There is great sensitivity here to ensuring that local residents and community will benefit from this new community. The Loreto Bay Company estimates that a thousand local jobs (long-term) have been created, and the restoration of the estuary bodes well for enhancing fishing prospects for this fishing village. Research suggests that for every hectare (2.5 acres) of restored mangrove estuary, a ton (0.9 metric ton) of marketable fish per year is generated. The restored Loreto Bay wetland system should generate 40 tons (36 metric tons) of marketable fish per year for local fisheries.

The approach taken to stormwater management and the emphasis placed on restoration of the estuary provide significant resilience benefits. The developed areas have been graded to send stormwater to the golf course, which acts as a large retention area. The restoration efforts along the estuary, including the planting of thousands of mangroves, will further enhance the ability of the landscape and community to absorb a major coastal storm.

Coastal resilience, then, is strengthened here in several ways: the restored and renewed estuary and coastal ecosystems will make the community more resilient in the face of storms, flooding, and other hazards; nurturing an economy built around local resources will enhance economic resilience; and the many sustainability aspects and features such as wind energy, low-energy homes, and water conservation and reuse will reduce the ecological footprint of the community and at the same time reduce the potential impact of forces from outside the community (e.g., declining global oil supplies).

For more information on the Villages at Loreto Bay, see www.loretobay.com.

Kinston, North Carolina: Sustainable Redevelopment and Green Infrastructure

The city of Kinston, North Carolina, offers an especially good example of a coastal community that has seen devastating natural disasters as an opportunity to become more resilient and sustainable.

Located in Lenoir County, in coastal North Carolina, Kinston has had to contend with serious flooding from the Neuse River. Not once, but twice the city has seen serious flooding from hurricanes—first, Hurricane Fran in 1996, and then Hurricane Floyd in 1999. The extent of the flooding and the amount of damage were substantial indeed.

To its credit, the city has worked hard to prevent rebuilding along the Neuse River and to relocate residents to safer locations outside the floodplain. In the end, the city and county purchased more than 1,600 homes in the floodplain. The results have been significant, with the majority (73 percent) of the floodplain within the city now undeveloped. The value of relocation was demonstrated in Kinston much sooner than expected (or hoped). The city had purchased about a hundred properties damaged or destroyed by Hurricane Fran by the time Hurricane Floyd struck in 1999. Had they been rebuilt in exactly the same location following Fran, they would have incurred significant damage. The North Carolina Department of Emergency Management (NCDEM) estimates that more than $6 million in damages were prevented as a result of the relocations following Fran—an impressive financial benefit reaped by the mitigation program over a relatively short period of time (NCDEM 2002).

A central principle of community sustainability is to emphasize the reuse of existing buildings and sites in a community before undeveloped, or "greenfield," locations are taken, and here Kinston offers a positive example and model. A key aspect of Kinston's poststorm redevelopment strategy was to actively promote development sites within the city as opportunities for rebuilding or relocating out of high-flood risk areas. The city prepared a comprehensive map that showed existing subdivisions where vacant parcels and building sites could be found, and generally took an active approach in helping relocated families stay within the town.

Convincing residents in the floodplain that moving back to these sites would be inadvisable and that alternatives were available became easier in Kinston because of the way rebuilding approval was organized. The city restricted access to the area of damaged homes by requiring an entry pass. These passes had to be collected at a building that also housed the buyout program. Homeowners were in essence provided "one-stop shopping" and were actively counseled about where else they might like to live.

An initiative called Call Kinston Home, which brought together a number of partners (including the city of Kinston, Lenoir County, NCDEM, and the North Carolina Homebuilders Association, among others), sought to encourage and facilitate urban development and redevelopment within existing neighborhoods and on in-fill lots, as well as in Kinston's downtown area. Among the strategies employed, the city provided a $10,000 grant to families in the floodplain to relocate within the city. Together these incentives and grassroots efforts at expanding housing opportunities within the city were successful, with the vast majority of floodplain households (some 98 percent) relocating back in the city.

One of the steps Kinston took was to take the rebuilding following Hurricane Floyd and the relocation out of and away from the floodplain as an opportunity to promote the reuse of older buildings in the city. Specifically, it has been working hard to interest developers in redeveloping several existing older buildings and properties, including the 4-acre (1.6-hectare) site of the city's former Grainger High School, a 1920s structure sitting abandoned at the time of Hurricane Floyd. With the use of low-income and historic tax credits, and FEMA disaster assistance funds, the high school has been renovated and reused as an elder housing project called Grainger Place. The developer also took advantage of financial incentives provided by the city. The result is a positive step in the direction of a more sustainable and resilient development pattern—in this case fifty-seven affordable units of elderly housing outside the flood hazard zone that preserved a significant public building and helped to strengthen the city's downtown. Along with housing, the renovated high school also includes a performing arts center, gym, and day care facility.

The city has also benefited from the preparation of two different green infrastructure plans created by groups of planning students at the University of North Carolina. The most recent, prepared in 2002, conveys what the city sees for the future of its floodplain—namely, as a tourism and recreational amenity for the city and region.

Solara: Solar-Powered Affordable Housing in San Diego County, California

In spring 2007, an innovative green affordable housing complex located in the city of Poway, in northern San Diego County, California, was completed. A collaboration between Community HousingWorks, a nonprofit housing developer, the Poway Redevelopment Agency, and Global Green USA, the complex will be the first net-zero-energy housing in California. This fifty-six-apartment complex will

FIGURE 13.2
Solara, in San Diego, is billed as the first affordable housing project in the United States fully powered by the sun.
Photo by Timothy Beatley.

be 100 percent powered by rooftop photovoltaics, at times sending more power into the grid than it needs (thus "net-zero energy"). Under the county's innovative "zero utility allowance," residents, who are able to rent the apartments at substantially below market rates, will have no energy bills to pay. The rooftops of this multiunit housing contain 141 kilowatts of photovoltaic panels, and per the conditions of the city, cannot be seen from street level (fig. 13.2).

The apartments incorporate a number of other green elements, including nontoxic paints, energy-efficient appliances, water-saving plumbing, recycled materials, and a landscape plan that includes no-mow grass, native tree species, and a citrus grove. The complex also includes a community center and office space and is located near public transit. Residents are encouraged to walk to nearby shops, and each unit has been given its own metal shopping cart. Community Housing Works has also commissioned the preparation of a green curriculum for the community and a green management/maintenance guide, and requires all residents to attend a brief pre-occupancy meeting about the green features of the neighborhood.

The photovoltaic panels added $1.1 million to the cost of the project but were funded in creative ways. Financing was provided in part through the California Energy Commission's Zero Energy New Homes Program's federal solar energy tax credit. One innovative aspect of the financing was the participation of the National Equity Fund, which raised a significant part of the funding ($208,000) for the photovoltaics by syndicating equity (selling investments in the business tax credits).

Global Green (2007, 1) points out the ultimate green benefits from Solara:

> The end result: SOLARA has the lowest carbon footprint of any apartment complex in California, 95 percent lower than a conventionally powered community, avoiding more than 1800 tons of carbon dioxide each year. That is the equivalent to planting 5,446 trees or taking 300 cars off the road annually.

Art is also a key feature of this project, and two artists were hired to create artworks throughout. These works include dramatic "sunquilts" that swivel in the wind and grace the entrance to the neighborhood. There is also a "Recyclescope," a kaleidoscope made of recycled materials, and an "Hour Glass," a rotatable water jug, both inside the community center. Outside, the art is everywhere, including underfoot. A series of "impression disks" have been implanted in the walkways and outdoor spaces, fourteen of them in all. These are textured images that are intended to allow kids in the neighborhood to make rubbings from them. There is a spider, and even a disk in the shape of the watershed in which the project lies. These elements of public art help to create a distinctive and interesting neighborhood, enhance the quality of living there, and perhaps in small ways strengthen bonds between residents, which in turn will help to promote resilience.

Maui County, Hawaii: Resilient Island Paradise

Maui County consists of three main islands, Maui, Molokai, and Lanai, and one smaller island, Kahoolawe—together known as Maui Nui ("greater Maui"). The bulk of the population and urban development are on Maui, whose economic engines are plantation agriculture and tourism. The 2005 resident population of Maui County was 140,050, most of it on the island of Maui (pop. 129,471). Forecasts for 2030 show substantial increases in both resident population and island visitors (Maui County 2008, 28).

Planning in Hawaii is unique compared with other American states. All land is classified at the state level into one of four categories: conservation, agricultural, rural, and urban. In Maui County, 94 percent of the zoning districts fall into either the conservation or the agricultural land use categories (Maui County 2008, 26); Of the county's 4 million acres (1.6 million hectares), only about 200,000 acres (about 81,000 hectares), or about 5 percent, are considered urban.

County planning occurs at multiple levels. A Countywide Policy Plan (a 2007 draft currently exists; see Maui County 2008) sets vision, goals, and broad policy, to be followed by more detailed island community plans for Molokai, Maui, and Lanai islands and several more focused plans for communities on Maui, the most populous island.

The state of Hawaii requires a minimum coastal setback of 25 feet (40 feet for deeper lots), but counties can increase this amount if they wish. Maui County has done so and has increased the setback to 25 feet, plus 50 times the annual erosion rate for specific island shorelines. Only minor activities or removable structures are permitted within this setback zone (e.g., movable public access walkways, landscape plantings, and movable lighting).

Planning in Maui has occurred through extensive public participation, including a process called Focus Maui Nui that in 2003 engaged 1,700 residents in "intensive, small-group participatory sessions" to identify key planning issues that helped form the vision expressed in the Maui Countywide Policy Plan. This 2030 policy plan lays out a vision statement that reflects Maui County's unique sense of place (see box 13.1).

Box 13.1 Maui County Vision

- Maui County will be an innovative model of sustainable island living and a place where every individual can grow to reach his or her potential.
- The needs of each individual, the needs of the whole community, and the needs of our natural and cultural assets will be brought into balance to reflect the high value we place on both our natural environment and our people.
- The education and health of our people will be fostered to ensure that the residents of these islands can, if they choose, spend their whole lives here— raising children, owning homes, enjoying rewarding jobs, and taking advantage of opportunities to contribute to this community and to be good stewards of our local treasures and resources.
- Maui County will be a leader in the creation of responsible, self-sufficient communities and environmentally sound economic development and land stewardship.
- That which makes Maui County unique in the world will be preserved, celebrated, and protected for generations to come.

Source: Maui County 2008, 1.

Natural hazards receive prominent mention in the 2030 plan, including a discussion of sea level rise. The plan states that an increase of as much as 3 meters (ca. 10 feet) might be experienced by 2030, and so will impact all shorelines. "Prudent planning will consider likely sea level rise as a variable in planning the island's future" (Maui County 2008, 18).

An island community, Maui is heavily dependent on goods and resources from the mainland, and a desire to be more self-sufficient has emerged strongly in the planning process. The 2030 plan reflects this concern, as can be seen in the following passage:

Maui is extremely dependent upon off-shore sources for energy, food, construction materials and common daily goods. The participants of Focus Maui Mio expressed a desire to retool the County's economy to enable Hawaii to be more self-reliant. This would mean expanding the agriculture, aquaculture, manufacturing and energy production on the islands. By working toward self-sufficiency, Maui County's economy could diversify dramatically, thereby offering additional opportunities for employment and income. In addition the offshore dollars that come into the County through the tourism industry add to Maui's economy, as the money earned in this export industry would purchase locally grown and produced goods and local services. (Maui County 2008, 38)

The Countywide Policy Plan goes on to identify a series of goals, objectives, and more specific policies, many of which address sustainability in some way or another. Indeed, promoting sustainable land use planning and development and strengthening the local economy are two of the plan's overarching strategies.

In the Maui plan, a compact, mixed-use land use is embraced in a number of places, along with the desire to guide future growth into those locations where infrastructure already exists. The plan calls for providing incentives for the production of local renewable energy ("solar, wind, hydro, agricultural bio-products and other sources of renewable energy"), under the objective of making the county less dependent on energy imports. Goal G, "Promote Sustainable Land Use Planning and Development," is the clearest and strongest expression of the plan's sustainable focus. More specific policies include establishing urban and rural growth limits, encouraging redevelopment and infill of existing communities, and use of transfer of development rights "to concentrate new development around existing infrastructure and services, and protect natural, scenic, shoreline and cultural resources" (p. 60).

The plan establishes a goal aimed at the kind of self-reliant economy it wants to see: "Maui County's economy will be diverse, sustainable, and favorable to small business" (p. 62). The plan proposes regulations and programs that permit local farmers and craftsmen to sell directly to the public, and to generate support regarding the purchasing of local products and steps to help diversify the county's economic base.

The county has also prepared a hazard mitigation plan that much more explicitly tackles natural hazards. Completed in 2006, this plan explicitly embraces sustainable communities and community resilience.

Maui has an extensive history of coastal storms; inland or stream flooding; high surf ("sudden high waves combined with strong near shore currents"); dam breaks; landslides; coastal erosion; seismic and tsunami hazards (95 tsunamis have been experienced over the course of 175 years, causing the greatest loss of life among all the hazards experienced there); drought; and wildfires (Maui County 2006). Major tsunami events causing extensive damage occurred in 1946 and 1960 (33-foot [ca. 10-meter] waves were seen on the northern coast of Maui during the 1946 tsunami).

A detailed Hazards Risk and Vulnerability Assessment was prepared utilizing the National Oceanic and Atmospheric Administration's Community Vulnerability Assessment Tool. Three criteria were used to prioritize hazards on the island: frequency of the hazard, area impacted by the hazard, and severity, result-ing in the highest score assigned to tsunamis, hurricanes, and coastal erosion. The plan also provides an extensive discussion and analysis of social vulnerability, vul-nerability of critical facilities, and more detailed vulnerability analysis for differ-ent types of hazards.

Chapter VI of the plan identifies mitigation actions and projects by type of hazard. A key table in the assessment presents a summary of proposed mitigation actions to address seismic threat. These are then assessed and evaluated (against so-called STAPLEE [social, technical, administrative, political, legal, economic, and environmental] criteria), and high priority projects are identified. An imple-mentation section is also included.

Noisette, North Charleston, South Carolina: Large-Scale Coastal Redevelopment with Resilience and Sustainability at the Core

Noisette is a large and ambitious master-planned redevelopment in North Charleston, designed around sustainability principles and undertaken through an extensive process of community engagement and consultation. Indeed, it is described as the "most ambitious plan for sustainable urban redevelopment in the nation's history," and this assessment seems not too far-fetched. The brainchild of innovative developer John Knott (known for his ecological plan for Dewees Island; see Beatley, Brower, and Schwab 2002), Noisette holds much promise as a positive model for sustainable and resilient redevelopment of coastal areas.

The development encompasses an area of about 3,000 acres (ca. 1,200 hectares) of North Charleston, including 350 acres (ca. 142 hectares) of the former North Charleston naval base (navy yard). Many of the existing structures on the naval base will be adaptively reused, providing some five to seven thousand dwelling units, and 6 to 10 million square feet (560 to 930 thousand square meters) of commer-cial and office space. The navy yard will serve as the redevelopment's "urban core": an area of mixed use where many of the existing base structures will be reused. Already some interesting activities are taking place in these base buildings, includ-ing studio space for local artists and the unusual American College of Building Arts, one of the few schools where one can train to become a stonemason, finish carpenter, or other building artisan.

Redevelopment of the navy yard is governed by an impressive design guide mandating green rooftops for new structures and integrated stormwater management. Noisette is utilizing innovative stormwater management techniques throughout. Only native plants are permitted, and specific bicycle parking standards are stipulated (a minimum of one space for every twenty auto spaces). (For more information about Noisette and for detailed maps and reports, see www.noisettesc.com.)

All buildings at Noisette will be green, and, specifically, all new commercial and institutional structures must have LEED (Leadership in Energy and Environmental Design) certification. Noisette has also developed its own set of green design standards for new residential construction. Working with the Atlanta-based nonprofit Southface, these design criteria, known as the Noisette Quality Home Standard, are specially adapted to the climate and conditions of the South Carolina low country.

The project also explicitly considers natural hazards. Knott explains that the entire development has been designed to withstand a category 5 hurricane as well as likely seismic forces. (For a complete explanation of the hurricane ranking system, see www.nhc.noaa.gov/aboutsshs.shtml.)

Noisette has also had a positive influence on green building throughout North Charleston. The new North Charleston elementary school is LEED certified, for instance, and the school district has now adopted a policy of minimum LEED certification for all new school buildings. A Sustainability Institute has been created, and a model Green House showcases many green living and building ideas and has already been instrumental in educating residents about these issues.

Ecological restoration is a major part of the Noisette concept, and a separate Noisette preserve plan has been prepared. Restoration of Noisette Creek, which runs through the project site and drains into the Cooper River, is a centerpiece of the project (about 135 acres, or about 55 hectares, overall). The plan identifies a critical buffer and new stormwater management features (bioswales), an interpretive nature center, walking and biking trails, and a native plants nursery. The plan envisions undertaking a number of restoration measures, including removal of nonnative and invasive species, the replanting of native tree species, removal of fill, and the reestablishment of wetlands in certain areas. The plan also identifies how, through a network of trails and pathways, the creek will connect to the larger neighborhood. The Michaux Conservancy and Land Trust has been formed to manage and steward over the preserve (and is a program area under the Noisette Foundation; see Noisette Company 2003).

The goal of the Noisette Creek restoration, and the Michaux Conservancy, is "reconnecting the local population with nature," and for the creek to serve as an outdoor classroom and research laboratory (Noisette Foundation 2007, 4). The creek is viewed as a significant educational resource for the fourteen schools located within 2 miles (3.2 kilometers), and it is imagined that the students will visit, learn about, and hopefully steward over this preserve. A Center for Urban Coastal Ecosystems, based at the creek preserve, is also envisioned.

What is especially impressive and different about what Knott and the Noisette Company espouse is the importance placed on community building and efforts to help reweave a strong social fabric in North Charleston. This focus may be as critical as anything in promoting resilience. Though Knott does not often use the word *resilience*, creating resilience is largely what he is doing.

This community building and engagement is also a matter of social and economic justice, Knott believes, and Noisette aims to include groups that have often been left out or left behind. Its support for the Lowcountry HUB Academy is an example of this inclusiveness. HUB stands for "historically underutilized businesses," and the idea is to offer an educational and training program aimed at minority businesses to help them to better market and sell goods and services to area contractors. The academy has recently graduated its fourth class, and there is every indication that this program will help expand income and revenue for these minority companies and will also enhance their efficiency and overall profitability.

The strong emphasis on place is also exemplary. Knott believes that a love of place is essential. The planning and development of Noisette, for instance, was preceded by an unusually deep examination of the history and natural features of the site. Even the name Noisette follows a nuanced and rich site history, named after Fleet Noisette, an eighteenth-century botanist who lived in the area.

Noisette is already in the process of developing one residential neighborhood, Oak Terrace Preserve, that reflects Noisette's emphasis on ecological restoration and green design. The development contains 303 residential lots (many with accessory units), 74 townhomes, and 17 pocket parks. Here, natural stormwater management techniques are incorporated in the form of linear bioswales 15 feet (4.5 meters) in width running alongside the roads and planted with native plant species, and through rain gardens located in alleys behind the homes. A set of design guidelines have also been prepared that specify design of architectural features of the homes (porches, exterior color, and materials); limit the amount of turf (no more than 20 percent of the lot); and strongly recommend that 75 percent of the plants used in home landscaping be South Carolina natives. Most dramatically, Oak Terrace has sited the new homes to minimize the loss of trees—in this case, the spectacular and large live oak trees. According to Knott, this sensitive site plan has saved 560 of the 700 trees originally on the location.

These shorter cases further demonstrate that there are many things that can be done to help push coastal communities in the direction of greater resilience. There are many more arrows in the coastal planner's quiver than is perhaps commonly thought. Many of these stories are of places and developments that are tackling natural hazards (tornadoes, coastal storms, tsunamis), but many are aimed at advancing broader resilience goals, such as reducing energy and resource consumption (e.g., Noisette and Solara); strengthening local economy (e.g., Maui); restoring coastal ecosystems (e.g., Villages at Loreto Bay); and expanding recreation and tourism opportunities (e.g., Kinston). Resilience, sustainability, and hazard mitigation, as chapter 1 argued, are indeed complementary and reinforcing goals, and these brief cases are strong evidence of that.

CONCLUSION

The Promise of Coastal Resilience

THAT COASTAL COMMUNITIES AND REGIONS around the world will face unprecedented challenges, especially from global warming and sea level rise, is perhaps obvious but can hardly be overstated. The challenges to effectively adapting to this new world will be not only physical in nature, but also profoundly economic, social, and cultural. In the decades ahead, coastal planners will find it even harder, though not impossible, to at once sustain higher levels of population and property safely and a high quality of life.

This book has examined the promise of resilience as a central organizing concept for guiding coastal planning and management for a possible calamitous future. Perhaps more than any competing notion, resilience offers an especially relevant and useful perspective on how to design, plan, and manage coastal communities. Although the term *resilience* is subject to a variety of specific definitions, its intuitive essence— the concept of designing and living in places that can effectively adapt to and relatively easily "bounce back" from storms and other shocks—has much appeal. In contrast, much of historic planning and policy has reflected a more rigid approach to living along the coast, with resistance and armoring the more common outcome.

Perhaps green architect William McDonough (2002) has the most apt metaphor for how we should be building and living in coastal areas. He speaks eloquently of the need to design buildings that function like trees—they produce all the power they need from the sun; they also produce oxygen and provide shade and cooling; they retain stormwater and are profoundly restorative as they replenish and stabilize the soil; and they provide many species with home and habitat. And, like most trees, they *bend* in the wind, and are highly resilient. Of course, trees are literally quite valuable in designing sustainable, resilient communities, but they also offer an excellent metaphor and image to keep in mind when envisioning the future of coastal environments.

The contours and specifics of this metaphorical tree are open to discussion, but this book has sought to make the case that there are indeed many steps we can take today, and many ways we can plan and design coastal communities to be much more resilient in the future. There is no one single thing to be done, but rather many things that need doing together—for instance, strengthening social networks and helping to build social capital; diversifying the local economy and working with the business community to build resilient and adaptive business models; protecting and restoring critical natural systems to protect communities in the face of climate change; and changing physical land use at local and regional levels—especially steps to move people and structures out of and away from the most dangerous locations, ones that will likely be subject to sea level rise and hurricane flooding.

Like the tree, every action we take, everything we build, every public investment we make in the future must accomplish multiple goals at once. Resilience suggests, for instance, a profoundly new way of thinking about coastal infrastructure, one that understands that many needs must be addressed. New neighborhood streets, for instance, can be designed not just as infrastructure to convey car traffic, but rather reimagined to incorporate community gathering places (and perhaps places for meeting and staging before or after disaster events) and to facilitate community interaction, as well as to collect and treat stormwater (bioswales and rain gardens), to grow food, to provide shading and climate benefits, and perhaps even to produce power. Every new community park might be viewed as an opportunity to enhance community resilience—for instance, by retaining floodwaters, by growing community food, and by providing opportunities and encouragement for physical activity. New schools might be designed with a range of resilience goals in mind: again, they can produce power; collect rainwater and provide drinking water following a devastating hurricane; and provide a healthy, daylight shelter and space for short-term housing when needed by the community. These are just a few of the new ways we need to reenvision community building and infrastructure through the lens of coastal resilience.

Coastal resilience will also require simultaneous action at a number of geographical or design scales. As argued in this book, much can be accomplished at the level of building design, but also very important steps can be taken in and around the building, and also at the neighborhood level—for example, more resilient, decentralized stormwater management; edible landscaping; and landscaping chosen for resilience. But much must also happen at city and regional levels, including land use planning that keeps development out of the riskiest high-inundation areas; preserving and restoring regional networks of green infrastructure; and planning for evacuation and sheltering. Much can be accomplished at each scale, but effective coastal resilience will require concerted action *at all scales*, ideally resulting in an interlocked and multiscaled resilient region.

The many stories and vignettes of how communities have successfully adapted in the face of catastrophe, such as New Orleans' Vietnamese neighborhood of Versailles after Hurricane Katrina, emphasize that in planning for resilience, the social and cultural aspects of a community are as important as the physical ones. We must do more thinking about what is needed to grow a more resilient culture over the long term. Stories such as the Terranova family's efforts to quickly reopen their community market after Katrina, and to stock the food and other items most needed in their community, demonstrate the critical importance of understanding the role that individuals, families, and community businesses can play in enhancing resilience.

Much of this interpersonal and neighborhood resilience will require a sense of commitment to community and place that is today, unfortunately, mostly absent in U.S. communities. How to rebuild this commitment, how to restitch a network of helping, caring citizens embedded in places they are committed to staying in and shepherding over will be one of our greatest challenges in the future.

The significance of place has probably not received enough attention in this book. The context of place—the history, landscape, and unique and special qualities of place, the climate and unique environment, and the shared cultural understandings—is the backdrop of coastal living and the real and tangible tableau in which every resilient action occurs. Place could and should be a much stronger element in any effort at shaping more sustainable and resilient coastal communities. The local climate should be the starting point in understanding how buildings can be designed to incorporate fresh air and daylight, to minimize energy and resource demands, and to be livable following a storm or disaster event ("passive survivability," as discussed in this book). As well, the landscape and biophysical context of a place at once shapes the feel and flavor of that place, and can through appreciating and preserving (and restoring) those qualities make the community more resilient. Resilience and place strengthening go hand in hand. And, in turn, the steps that help to nurture stronger place commitments yield dividends in enhancing the ability and likelihood that, when the need arises, residents and neighbors will step forward to help others and the larger community. Place commitments, then, are critical to coastal resilience.

There are many obstacles to growing more resilient coastal communities and regions, a number of which have been examined in these chapters—for instance, the often lower priority given to longer-term and more catastrophic events (e.g., Category 5 hurricanes); the short-term bias of local electoral cycles that emphasize the visible and the concrete; and the difficulty of any action that might be perceived as disrupting local growth or interfering with private property rights. Moving forward in creating the conditions for truly resilient coastal communities will require efforts to tackle some or all of these obstacles. A new sort of political leader will be needed—for instance, one with an expanded ethical viewpoint about the importance of steps that will make the entire community safer over a much longer period of time (i.e., hundreds of years!), and a recognition of the need to sometimes sublimate the short-term-profit demands of individuals. Climate change will require courageous steps and expeditious and often herculean actions and, in turn, elected officials who are able to rise to these circumstances and to exhibit a degree of leadership and personal humility that is often lacking. How to grow these new leaders, with these new ethical sensibilities, is a major question.

Courageous, forward-looking coastal leaders in turn depend on supportive constituents and community groups who see for themselves the value of long-term resilience. Thus education, awareness raising, and community forums of various kinds to openly and candidly discuss future threats and challenges (as well as opportunities) will be essential. Getting many things done to enhance resilience will require partnerships and the joining together of sometimes warring community factions in common support of a larger and longer-term community good (again back to the importance of community discourse and candid discussion of the natural forces and challenges faced by the community).

These challenges and obstacles may seem daunting, and the tone of these concluding remarks too negative. But it is useful to return to an observation made in the book's introduction—that coastal resilience need not be cast in the pejorative; it need not be viewed as a mostly negative, costly, and sacrificial set of steps that are necessary, given the times, but not especially exciting or valuable in themselves. Actually, the contrary is more likely true. Designing new homes and buildings that

provide abundant daylight and fresh air, that utilize natural and local building materials, and that are able to produce at least some of the power they need offers the
hope of healthier, more enjoyable living. Developing programs for growing more
food locally and regionally offers tremendous benefits in terms of taste, freshness,
and connectedness to place, among other important values. Growing new community institutions and nurturing new social capital to make a community and
region more resilient has perhaps its primary value and benefit at the level of personal connectedness—stronger friendships and social bonds will make us more
resilient, but, perhaps most importantly, they make for a more meaningful, healthy
life. For the most part, then, coastal resilience has the potential to pay large returns
in the form of higher quality of life and personal and family enrichment. At the
end of the day, resilience is not about sacrifice so much as what is necessary for a
safe, sustainable, and meaningful life for all coastal residents over a long arc of time.

Appendix I:
Passive Survivability:
A Checklist for Action

Create storm-resilient buildings.

Design and construct buildings to withstand reasonably expected storm events and flooding. One should assume that storm events will become more common and more intense in the future, and that regions prone to severe storms will expand in area. More stringent design and construction standards, such as the Miami-Dade County Building Code, should be adopted widely.

Limit building height.

Most tall buildings, with their dependence on electrically powered elevators and their reliance on air conditioning, usually cannot be used in the event of power outages. The occupant density in tall buildings generally precludes providing a significant fraction of power requirements with onsite renewable sources, and in a development pattern with a lot of tall buildings, blocking solar access of other buildings is a significant concern. In *Adapting Buildings and Cities for Climate Change*, the authors recommend six to eight stories as a reasonable height limit.

Create a high-performance envelope.

High levels of insulation, high-performance glazings (with multiple low-emissivity coatings and low-conductivity gas fill), and airtight construction are critical in achieving passive survivability in buildings. High levels of energy performance of the envelope (superinsulation) are particularly important with smaller, skin-dominated buildings.

Minimize cooling loads.

Reduce unwanted solar heat gain by paying careful attention to building orientation (situating buildings on an east-west axis with the long façades facing south and north), minimizing east- and west-facing glazings, specifying glazings "tuned" to the orientation (using low solar-heat-gain-coefficient glazings on the east and west, for example), using overhangs and other building geometry features to shade glazings, and selecting vegetative plantings that will shade the buildings (particularly the east and west façades).

Provide for natural ventilation.

In addition to reducing unwanted solar gain, design buildings to provide for natural ventilation. Even if the building is designed to operate with conventional air conditioning, provide operable windows, natural stack-effect cooling towers, and other features that can provide passive ventilation and cooling when necessary—even if using such strategies will result in higher-than-desired humidity levels in the building.

Incorporate passive solar heating.

Particularly with smaller, skin-dominated buildings, provide passive solar design features, such as direct solar gain with interior thermal mass, thermal storage walls (Trombe walls), and sunspaces or other isolated-gain solar systems.

Provide natural daylighting.

The following strategies can optimize daylighting design while minimizing unwanted heat gain: provide windows high on exterior walls; specify glazings with high visible-light transmission and a low solar-heat-gain coefficient; install light-shelves to reflect light deep into the space; install skylights with provisions to prevent overheating; paint ceilings and walls with high-reflectance paints; consider clerestory windows and light monitors to bring light deep into buildings; utilize light wells and atria to extend daylighting to lower floors of larger buildings; in buildings with very deep floorplates, consider light-scoop and mirror systems to improve daylight distribution in the interior space.

Provide solar water heating.

To provide hot water during power outages or fuel supply interruptions, install solar water heating systems that can operate passively (thermosiphoning or batch/integral-collector-storage) or that operate with DC pumps powered by integrated photovoltaic (PV) modules.

Provide photovoltaic power.

Capability to power a building with PVs is invaluable during outages. To be able to rely on PV power during a power outage for nighttime electricity necessitates battery storage, which increases system cost substantially (but may be justified for the value provided). Be sure to mount PV modules in a manner that will protect them during storms. Wire the building to isolate critical loads so that they can be PV powered when the rest are cut off.

Configure heating equipment to operate on PV power.

The vast majority of gas- and oil-fired heating equipment cannot operate without electricity. Providing the capability to operate that equipment during a power outage—using either a generator or a PV power system—is clearly beneficial. To simplify switching over to PV operation during an outage, equipment should be redesigned to operate on DC power; even without battery storage, some operation of heating equipment would be possible during a 24-hour period.

Where appropriate, consider wood heat.

In more rural areas, install low-pollution-emitting wood stoves, masonry heaters, or pellet stoves (with back-up power for fan) to provide space heating in the event of an extended power outage or fuel-supply interruption.

Store water on site; consider using rainwater to maintain a cistern.

Provide water storage to serve the building during an extended loss of water. Ideally, store this water high in the building, such as on the rooftop, to facilitate gravity delivery. In cohousing communities and planned neighborhoods, shared water systems can be developed with gravity-feed to dwellings. Cisterns can be fed with rainwater and used during normal building operation for landscape irrigation and, depending on local permitting, for toilet flushing—as long as an adequate reservoir is maintained for emergency use. Such cisterns can also serve fire suppression needs.

Install composting toilets and waterless urinals.

Composting toilets and waterless urinals can be used in the event of water loss, and composting toilets can function even if the municipal sewage treatment plant shuts down. In a large building with conventional toilets, such as an apartment building, consider installing one or two high-capacity composting toilets in a common area for use if water supply is cut off or the sewer system fails.

Provide for food production in the site plan.

Whenever possible, provide for local food production in the site planning for a building or development. Consider setting aside the best land for agricultural uses and planting food-bearing trees and shrubs in the landscaping mix.

Source: Reprinted with permission from *Environmental Building News*™ May 2006 issue (Volume 15 Number 6). *EBN* is a publication of BuildingGreen, LLC located in Brattleboro, VT. For more information go to BuildingGreen.com

REFERENCES

Allen, Jeffrey, and Kang Lu. 2003. "Modeling and Prediction of Future Urban Growth in the Charleston Region of South Carolina: A GIS-Based Integrated Approach." *Conservation Ecology* 8 (2): 2. http://www.strom.clemson.edu/teams/dctech/urban.html; accessed February 4, 2009.

[ASLA] American Society of Landscape Architects. 2008. "Landscape Structures Commits $200,000 to Sustainable Sites Initiative." Press release, June 17. Washington, DC: ASLA.

Baker, Earl J., Robert E. Deyle, Timothy S. Chapin, John B. Richardson. 2008. "Are We Any Safer? Comprehensive Plan Impacts on Hurricane Evacuation and Shelter Demand in Florida," *Coastal Management* 36 (3): 294–317.

Barker, Jeff. 2003. "Recovery and Remembrance: A Year after the Storm, La Plata Residents Mark Their Progress in Rebuilding." *Washington Post*, April 27.

Beatley, Timothy. 2005.*Native to Nowhere: Sustaining Home and Community in a Global Age.* Washington, DC: Island Press.

Beatley, Timothy, David J. Brower, and Anna Schwab. 2002. *An Introduction to Coastal Zone Management.* 2nd ed. Washington, DC: Island Press.

Bell, Michelle L., Richard Goldberg, Christian Hogrefe, Patrick L. Kinney, Kim Knowlton, Barry Lynn, Joyce Rosenthal, Cynthia Rosenzweig, and Jonathan A. Patz. 2007. "Climate Change, Ambient Ozone, and Health in 50 U.S. Cities." *Climatic Change* 82:61–76.

Bender, Tom. 2001. "Building Community Sustainability: Bank of Astoria." http://www.tombender.org/sustdesignarticles/Bank_of_Astoria.pdf; accessed February 4, 2009.

Berke, Philip R., and Thomas J. Campanella. 2006. "Planning for Postdisaster Resiliency." *Annals of the American Academy of Political and Social Science* 604: 192–207.

Briggs, Xavier de Souza. 2004. "Social Capital: Easy Beauty or Meaningful Resource?" *Journal of the American Planning Association* 70 (2): 151–58.

Buckle, Philip. 2006. "Assessing Social Resilience." In Paton and Johnston 2006a, 88–104.

Burby, Raymond J. 2003. "Making Plans That Matter: Citizen Involvement and Government Action." *Journal of the American Planning Association* 69 (1): 33–49.

———. 2005. "Have State Comprehensive Planning Mandates Reduced Insured Losses from Natural Disasters?" *National Hazard Review* 6: 67–81.

———. 2006. "Hurricane Katrina and the Paradoxes of Government Disaster Policy: Bringing About Wise Governmental Decisions for Hazardous Areas." *Annals of the American Academy of Political and Social Service* 604: 171–91.

Burby, Raymond J., and Peter J. May, eds. 1997. *Making Governments Plan: State Experiments in Managing Land Use.* Baltimore: Johns Hopkins University Press.

Butterfield, David. 2006. Presentation to the Gaining Ground Conference, June, Victoria, BC.

California Seismic Safety Commission. 2005. *The Tsunami Threat to California: Findings and Recommendations on Tsunami Hazards and Risks.* Sacramento: California Seismic Safety Commission.

Campanella, Thomas J. 2006. "Urban Resilience and the Recovery of New Orleans." *Journal of the American Planning Association Longer View* 72 (2): 141–46.

Charleston County, SC. 2004. *County of Charleston Comprehensive Plan.* October 5. Charleston, SC.

———. 2006. *Comprehensive Greenbelt Plan 2006–2030.* Adopted June 6. http://www.smallchangeforbigchange.org/greenbeltplan.html; accessed February 3, 2009.

———. 2008. *County of Charleston Comprehensive Plan*. Updated, Adopted November 18. http://www.charlestoncounty.org/departments/Planning/Comp_Plan.htm; accessed February 4, 2009.

———. n.d. "Hazard Resistant Landscaping." http://www.charlestoncounty.org/departments /BuildingServices/ProjectImpact/landscaping_Brochure.pdf; accessed February 4, 2009.

———. n.d. "Project Impact." http://www.charlestoncounty.org/departments/buildingservices /projectimpact.htm; accessed February 4, 2009.

City of Crisfield, MD. 2007. *Comprehensive Plan*. Prepared by Jakubiak and Associates, Inc., Crisfield, MD.

City of New Orleans. 2006. *Citywide Strategic Recovery and Rebuilding Plan*. New Orleans, LA.

City of Ocean City, MD. 2004. *Hazard Mitigation Plan*. Adopted July 27.

City of Portland, Bureau of Sustainability and Planning. n.d. "Ecoroofs." http://www.portlandon-line.com/osd/index.cfm?a=114728&c=42113; accessed February 4, 2009.

Columbia University, Center for Climate Systems Research. n.d. "Hurricanes, Sea Level Rise, and New York City." http://www.ccsr.columbia.edu/information/hurricanes; accessed February 4, 2009.

Costanza, Robert, William J. Mitsch, and John W. Day Jr. 2006. "A New Vision for New Orleans and the Mississippi Delta: Applying Ecological Economics and Ecological Engineering." *Frontiers in Ecology and the Environment* 4 (9): 465–72.

Crossett, Kristen M., Thomas J. Culliton, Peter C. Wiley, and Timothy R. Goodspeed. 2004. *Population Trends along the Coastal United States: 1980–2008*. Washington, DC: NOAA National Ocean Service. http://oceanservice.noaa.gov/programs/mb/pdfs/coastal_pop_trends _complete.pdf; accessed February 4, 2009.

Cutter, Susan L., ed. 2001. *American Hazard Scopes: The Regionalization of Natural Hazards and Disasters*. Washington, DC: Joseph Henry.

Cutter, Susan L., Bryan J. Boruff, and W. Lynn Shirley. 2003. "Social Vulnerability to Environmental Hazards." *Social Science Quarterly* 84 (2): 242–61.

Day, John W., Jr., John Barras, Ellis Clairain, James Johnston, Dubravko Justic, G. Paul Kemp, Jae-Young Ko, et al. 2005. "Implications of Global Climatic Change and Energy Cost and Availability for the Restoration of the Mississippi Delta." *Ecological Engineering* 24 (4): 253–65.

Dean, Cornelia. 2006. "Next Victim of Warming: The Beaches." *New York Times*, June 20, Science sec.

Disaster Safety.org. n.d. "Protecting Where You Live." http://www.disastersafety.org; accessed February 5, 2009.

Druyan, Leonard, Barry Lynn, and Richard Healy. 2007. "Precipitation and the Potential for Extreme Temperature Change." *Science Briefs*, NASA Goddard Institute for Space Studios, New York. http://www.giss.nasa.gov/research/briefs/druyan_07.

Easton, David, 1965. *A Systems Analysis of Political Life*. New York: Wiley.

Elazar, Daniel J. 1984. *American Federalism: A View from the States*. New York: Harper Collins.

Emanuel, Kerry. 2005a. *Divine Wind: The History and Science of Hurricanes*. New York: Oxford University Press.

———. 2005b. "Increasing Destructiveness of Tropical Cyclones over the Past 30 Years." *Nature* 436: 686–88.

Emergency Management Australia. 1998. Australian Emergency Management Glossary. Canberra: Emergency Management Australia.

Florida State University (FSU). 2008. "Warmer Seas Linked to Strengthening Hurricanes: FSU Study Fuels Global Warming Debate." Press release. http://www.fsu.edu/news/2008/09/03/warmer.seas; accessed February 4, 2009.

Girling, Cynthia L., and Ronald Kellett. 2005. *Skinny Streets and Green Neighborhoods: Design for Environment and Community*. Washington, DC: Island Press.

Global Green, 2007. "First Fully Solar-Powered Apartment Community in California Opens." http://www.globalgreen.org/press/34; accessed February 4, 2009.

Godschalk, David R. 2003. "Urban Hazard Mitigation: Creating Resilient Cities." *Natural Hazards Review* 4 (3): 136–43.

Godschalk, David R., Timothy Beatley, Philip Berke, David J. Brower, and Edward J. Kaiser. 1999. *Natural Hazard Mitigation: Recasting Disaster Policy and Planning*. Washington, DC: Island Press.

Godschalk, David R., David J. Brower, and Timothy Beatley. 1989. *Catastrophic Coastal Storms: Natural Hazard Mitigation and Development Management*. Durham, NC: Duke University Press.

Gornity, Vivien, Radley Horton, and Cynthia Rosenzweig. 2006. "Vulnerability of New York City to Storms and Sea Level Rise." *Geol. Soc. of America Abstract Programs*, no. 7, 335.

Greater Atlanta Home Builders Association and Southface. n.d. "EarthCraft House." http://www.earthcrafthouse.com; accessed February 4, 2009.

Gregg, Chris E., and Bruce F. Houghton. 2006. "Natural Hazards." In Paton and Johnston 2006a, 19–39.

Hansen, Jim. 2006. "The Threat to the Planet." *New York Review*, July 13. http://www.nybooks.com /articles/19131; accessed February 4, 2009.

———. 2007. "Huge Sea Level Rises Are Coming—Unless We Act Now." *New Scientist*, July 25. http://www.newscientist.com/article/mg19526141.600-huge-sea-level-rises-are-coming —unless-we-act-now.html?full=true&print=true; accessed February 4, 2009.

Harden, Bruce. 2007. "Oregon Rethinks Easing Land Use Limits: Trying to Untie Property Owners' Hands, Voters End Some Checks on Sprawl." *Washington Post*, March 11.

Heinberg, Richard. 2003. *The Party's Over: Oil, War and the Fate of Industrial Societies*. Gabriola Island, BC: New Society.

Hill, Lance. 2006. "The Miracle of Versailles: New Orleans Vietnamese Community Rebuilds." *Louisiana Weekly*, January 23.

Holling, Crawford Stanley. 1973. "Resilience and Stability of Ecological Systems." *Annual Review of Ecology and Systematics* 4: 1–23.

Hsu, Spencer S. 2007. "FEMA to Let Katrina Victims Move from Trailers into Hotels." *Washington Post*, September 5.

[IBHS] Institute for Home and Business Safety. 2005. *Fortified . . . for safer living Builder's Guide*. Florida ed. June.

———. n.d. *Fortified . . . for safer living*. http://www.ibhs.org/property_protection/default.asp?id=8; accessed February 4, 2009.

[IBHS/APA] Institute for Business and Home Safety/American Planning Association. 2007. "Summary of State Land Use Planning Laws." March. Tampa, FL: Institute for Business and Home Safety.

[IPCC] Intergovernmental Panel on Climate Change. 2007a. "Climate Change 2007: Impacts, Adaptation and Vulnerability: Summary for Policymakers." April. Geneva, Switzerland: IPCC.

———. 2007b. *IPCC Fourth Assessment Report, Working Group I Report: "The Physical Science Basis": Technical Summary*. Geneva, Switzerland: IPCC.

[ISO] Insurance Services Office. n.d. "ISO Mitigation Online." http://www.isomitigation.com; accessed February 4, 2009.

Jacob, Klaus, Vivien Gornitz, and Cynthia Rosenzweig. 2007. "Vulnerability of the New York City Metropolitan Area to Coastal Hazards, Including Sea-Level Rise: Inferences for Urban Coastal Risk Management and Adaptation Policies." In *Managing Coastal Vulnerability*, ed. L. McFadden, R. Nicholls, and E. Penning-Rowsell, 139–56. New York; Elsevier Science.

Johnston, David, Julia Becker, and Jim Cousins. 2006. "Lifelines and Urban Resilience." In Paton and Johnston 2006a, 40–65.

Land Trust Alliance. n.d. "2005 National Land Trust Census." http://www.landtrustalliance.org /about-us/land-trust-census; accessed February 4, 2009.

Lynn, Barry H., Richard Healy, and Leonard M. Druyan. 2007. "An Analysis of the Potential for Extreme Temperature Change Based on Observations and Model Simulations." *Journal of Climate* 15 (20): 1539–54.

Maryland Coastal Bays Program. n.d. *Maryland Coastal Bays Watershed Conservation and Management Plan: Setting a Course for the Future of our Community*. Ocean City, MD: Maryland Coastal Bays Program. http://www.mdcoastalbays.org; accessed February 4, 2009.

Maryland Department of Natural Resources. 2004. *State of the Maryland Coastal Bays*. Annapolis: State of Maryland.

Maui Coastal Land Trust. n.d. "History of the Maui Coastal Land Trust." http://www.mauicoastallandtrust.org/history.php; accessed February 4, 2009.

Maui County, 2006. *The Maui County Hazard Mitigation Plan*, Maui County.

———. 2008. Countywide Policy Plan Draft. http://www.co.maui.hi.us/index.asp?NID=420; accessed February 4, 2009.

McDonough, William, 2002. "Buildings Like Trees, Cities Like Forests." http://www.mcdonough.com/writings/buildings_like_trees.htm; accessed February 4, 2009.

McGranahan, Gordon, Deborah Balk, and Brigit Anderson. 2007. "The Rising Tide: Assessing the Risks of Climate Change and Human Settlements in Low Elevation Coastal Zones." *Environment and Urbanization* 19 (1): 17–37.

McPherson, Miller, Lynn Smith-Lovin, and Mathew Bashears. 2006. "Social Isolation in America: Changes in Core Discussion Networks over Two Decades." *American Sociological Review* 71 (June): 353–75.

Mileti, Dennis S. 1999. *Disasters by Design: A Reassessment of Natural Hazards in the United States.* Washington, DC: Joseph Henry.

[MMC] Multihazard Mitigation Council, 2005. *Natural Hazard Mitigation Saves: An Independent Study to Assess the Future Savings from Mitigation Activities.* Vol. 1, *Findings, Conclusions and Recommendations.* Washington, DC: National Institute of Building Sciences.

Moe, Richard. 1994. "Communities of Risk: The Consequences of Sprawl." *Historic Preservation News*, December–January.

Mortenson, E. 2007. "Measure 49 Scales Back Rural Housing Development." *Oregonian*, June 19. http://blog.oregonlive.com/breakingnews/2008/06/measure_49_will_scale_back_rur.html; accessed February 4, 2009.

[NASA] National Aeronautics and Space Administration. 2007. "NASA Study Suggests Extreme Summer Warming in the Future." New York: NASA Goddard Institute for Space Studies. http://www.giss.nasa.gov/research/news/20070509; accessed February 4, 2009.

[NCDEM] North Carolina Department of Emergency Management. 2002. "Kinston-Lenoir County Acquisition Project: Sustainable Development." Raleigh: NC Department of Emergency Management.

Nicholls, R. J., S. Hanson, C. Herweijer, N. Patmore, S. Hallegatte, Jan Corfee-Morlot, Jean Chateau, and R. Muir-Wood. 2007. *Ranking of the World's Cities Most Exposed to Coastal Flooding Today and in the Future.* London: OECD.

[NOAA] National Oceanic and Atmospheric Administration. n.d. "National Overview of Population Trends along the Coastal United States." http://oceanservice.noaa.gov/programs/mb/pdfs/2_national_overview.pdf; accessed February 4, 2009.

Noisette Company, 2003. *Noisette Community Masterplan.* Charleston, SC: Noisette Company.

———. 2005. *The Navy Yard at Noisette Design Guide.* North Charleston, SC: The Noisette Company.

Noisette Foundation. 2007. *The Michaux Conservancy: A Noisette Foundation Strategic Initiative for Ecosystem Education and Restoration.* Charleston, SC: Noisette Foundation.

Norris, Michelle. 2006. "Law Stands in the Way of Sturdy Katrina Cottages." National Public Radio, March 30. http://www.npr.org/templates/story/story.php?storyId=5313007; accessed February 4, 2009.

Nossiter, Adam, 2007a. "New Orleans Proposes to Invest in 17 Areas." *New York Times*, March 30, sec. A.

———. 2007b. "Steering New Orleans's Recovery with a Clinical Eye." *New York Times*, April 10.

Oregon Natural Hazards Workgroup. 2006. *Cannon Beach Post-Disaster Recovery Planning Forum, Cannon Beach, Oregon.* Eugene: Oregon Natural Hazards Workgroup.

Overpeck, Jonathan, Bette L. Otto-Bliesner, Gifford H. Miller, Daniel R. Muhs, Richard B. Alley, and Jeffrey T. Kiehl. 2006. "Paleoclimatic Evidence for Future Ice-Sheet Instability and Rapid Sea-Level Rise." *Science* 311 (March 24): 1747–50.

Overpeck, Jonathan, and Jeremy Weiss. n.d.. "Climate Change and Sea Level." http://www.geo.arizona.edu/dgesl/research/other/climate_change_and_sea_level/sea_level_rise/sea_level_rise_old.htm#images; accessed February 4, 2009.

Palm Beach County, Florida. 2004. *Unified Local Mitigation Strategy.* Rev. West Palm Beach: Palm Beach County.

———. 2005. *Palm Beach County Comprehensive Plan.* Rev. November 28. West Palm Beach: Palm Beach County.

———. 2006. *Countywide Post Disaster Redevelopment Plan, Palm Beach County, Florida.* West Palm Beach: Palm Beach County Division of Emergency Management. August. Paton, Douglas, 2006. "Disaster Resilience: Building Capacity to Co-Exist with Natural Hazards and Their Consequences." In Paton and Johnston 2006a, 3–10.

Paton, Douglas, and David Johnston. 2006a. *Disaster Resilience: An Integrated Approach*. Springfield, IL: CC Thomas.

———. 2006b. "Identifying the Characteristics of a Disaster Resilient Society." In Paton and Johnston 2006a, 1118.

Paton, Douglas, Gail Kelly, and Michael Doherty. 2006. "Exploring the Complexity of Social and Ecological Resilience to Hazards." In Paton and Johnston 2006a, 190–212.

Paton, Douglas, John McClure, and Petra T. Bürgelt. 2006. "Natural Hazard Resilience: The Role of Individual and Household Preparedness." In Paton and Johnston 2006a, 305–18.

Perlstein, Linda, and Amy Argetsinger. 2003. "Power Cords Link Haves, Have-Notes, Community Sharing Turns on Some Lights." *Washington Post*, September 21.

Pielke, Roger A., Jr. 2007. "Future Economic Damage from Tropical Cyclones: Sensitivities to Societal and Climate Changes." *Philosophical Transactions of the Royal Society* 365 (July): 2717–29

Pielke, Roger A., Jr., Joel Gratz, Christopher W. Landsea, Douglas Collins, Mark A. Saunders, and Rade Musuli. 2008. "Normalized Hurricane Damages in the United States: 1900–2005." *Natural Hazards Review* 9 (1): 29–42.

Pooley, J., L. Cohen, and M. O'Connor. 2006. "Links between Community and Individual Resilience: Evidence from Cyclone Affected Communities in North West Australia." In Paton and Johnston 2006a, 161–73.

Putnam, Robert D. 2000. *Bowling Alone: The Collapse and Revival of American Community*. New York: Simon & Schuster.

Putnam, Robert D., Lewis M. Feldstein, and Don Cohen. 2004. *Better Together: Restoring the American Community*. New York: Simon & Schuster.

Ridge, Kari K. 2003. "La Plata Residents, Businesses Rebuild After 2002 Tornado." Charles County Business. http://imagescharlescounty.com/index.php/site/articles/business/la_plata_residents _businesses_rebuild_after_2002_tornado; accessed February 4, 2009.

Rosenzweig, Cynthia, William Solecki, and Ronald B. Slosberg. 2006. "Mitigating New York City's Heat Island with Urban Forestry, Living Roofs, and Light Surfaces. New York: New York State Energy Research and Development Authority.

Save Our Cypress Campaign. n.d. *Action Manual*. http://healthygulf.org/images/stories/Cypress/save _our_cypress_action_manual.pdf.

Shaffrey, Mary. 2003. "'Life Goes On' in La Plata: Small Town Bands Together to Rebuild after April Tornado." *Washington Times*, December 22, sec. A.

Strange, Patrick. 2006. "Strength to Lead the Charge" *Times Picayune*, August 29.

Titus, James, and Charlie Richmond. 2001. "Maps of Lands Vulnerable to Sea Level Rise: Modeled Elevations along the U.S. Atlantic And Gulf Coasts." *Climate Research* 18: 205–28. http://www.epa.gov/climatechange/effects/coastal/slrmaps_vulnerable.html; accessed February 4, 2009.

Tobin, Graham A. 1999. "Community Resilience: The Holy Grail of Hazards Planning." *Environmental Hazards* 1: 13–26.

Tobin, Graham A., and Burrell E. Montz. 1997. *Natural Hazards: Explanation and Integration*. New York: Guilford.

Town of La Plata. 2001. *The Plan for the Future of Downtown La Plata: A Design for A New Downtown*. La Plata, MD: Town of La Plata.

Trenberth, Kevin E. 2007. "Warmer Oceans, Stronger Hurricanes." *Scientific American* (July): 45–51.

University of North Carolina, Department of City and Regional Planning. 2002. *Linking Natural and Historic Resources: Green Infrastructure as Economic Development in Lenoir County, NC*. Chapel Hill: University of North Carolina.

U.S. Army Corps of Engineers. 2004. *Louisiana Coastal Area (LCA) Ecosystem Restoration Study*. Vol. 1, New Orleans District. November. New Orleans; U.S. Army Corps of Engineers.

[USBC] U.S. Green Building Council. 2005. "The New Orleans Principles." http://green-reconstruction.buildinggreen.com/documents.attachment/305068/NewOrleans _Principles_LowRes.pdf; accessed February 4, 2009.

———. n.d. "What Is LEED?" http://www.usgbc.org/DisplayPage.aspx?CMSPageID=222; accessed February 4, 2009.

[USEPA] U.S. Environmental Protection Agency. n.d. "Energy Star New Homes." http://www.energystar.gov/index.cfm?c=new_homes.hm_index; accessed February 4, 2009.

Vale, Larry, and Thomas J. Campanella. 2005. *The Resilient City: How Modern Cities Recover from Disaster*. Oxford, England: Oxford University Press.

Venhaus, Heather. 2008. "Sustainable Sites Initiative." *Home Energy* (July/August). http://www.homeenergy.org.

Walker, Brian, Stephen Carpenter, John Anderies, Nick Abel, Graeme S. Cumming, Marco Janssen, Louis Lebel, Jon Norberg, Garry D. Peterson, and Rusty Pritchard. 2002. "Resilience Management in Social-Ecological Systems: A Working Hypothesis for a Participatory Approach." *Conservation Ecology* 6 (1): 14. http://www.ecologyandsociety.org/vol6/iss1/art14/#Terminology; accessed February 4, 2009.

Walker, Brian, S. Crawford, Stephen Holling, R. Carpenter, and Alan King. 2004. "Resilience, Adaptability and Transformability in Social-Ecological Systems." *Ecology and Society* 9 (2): 5.

Walker, Brian, and David Salt. 2006. *Resilience Thinking: Sustaining Ecosystems and People in a Changing World*. Washington, DC: Island Press.

Walsh, Mary L., with Justin Spencer. 2006. *Local Governments and Climate Change*. Washington, DC: ICMA.

Waugh, William L. 1990. "Emergency Management and the Capacities of State and Local Governments." In Richard T. Sylves and William L. Waugh, eds., *Cities and Disasters: North American Studies in Emergency Management*. Springfield, IL: CC Thomas.

Webster, P. J., G. J. Holland, J. A. Curry, and H.-R. Chang. 2005. "Changes in Tropical Cyclone Number, Duration and Intensity in a Warming Environment." *Science* 309: 1844–46.

Wilson, Alex. 2005. "Passive Survivability." *Environmental Building News* 14 (12). http://www.buildinggreen.com/auth/article.cfm/2005/12/1/Passive-Survivability; accessed February 4, 2009.

———. 2006. "Passive Survivability: A New Design Criterion for Buildings." *Environmental Building News*, May 1. http://www.buildinggreen.com/auth/article.cfm/ID/3342; accessed February 4, 2009.

Worcester County, MD. 2006a. *Comprehensive Development Plan*. March 7. www.co.worcester.md.us /cp/compindex.htm; accessed February 4, 2009.

———. 2006b. *Hazard Mitigation Plan*, September. Snow Hill, MD: Worcester County,

———. 2006c. *Worcester County Land Preservation, Parks and Recreation Plan*. Berlin, MD; Worcester County.

Worcester County Department of Recreation and Parks. 2006. *Worcester County Land Preservation Parks and Recreation Plan*. April 18. Snow Hill, MD: Worcester County.

Yardley, William. 2006. "Anger Drives Property Rights Measures, *New York Times*, October 8. http://query.nytimes.com/gst/fullpage.html?res=980DE5D71230F93BA35753C1A9609C8B63 &sec=&spon=&pagewanted; accessed February 4, 2009.

INDEX

Island Press | Board of Directors